C

Maggie McNie, MW, entered the wine trade by accident in 1974, having originally trained as an actress and studied classical singing with the great English tenor, Heddle Nash. In 1986 she passed the Master of Wine examination, and since then has worked as a wine consultant and speaker. She has contributed to various wine encyclopaedias, including the *Larousse* and the *Oxford Companion to Wine*. She is currently a director of Bacchus PR Ltd and still keeps in contact with her theatrical background as a board member of The Cherub Company, London.

FABER BOOKS ON WINE

Series Editor: Julian Jeffs

CHAMPAGNE

MAGGIE MCNIE

faber and faber
LONDON · NEW YORK

This book is dedicated to Colin Deane
without whose help and encouragement
it would never have been written.

First published in 1999
by Faber and Faber Limited
3 Queen Square London WCIN 3AU

Published in the United States by Faber and Faber Inc.,
a division of Farrar, Straus and Giroux Inc., New York

This paperback edition first published in 2000

Phototypeset by Intype London Ltd
Printed in England by Clays Ltd, St Ives plc

A CIP record for this book
is available from the British Library

ISBN 0-571-17469-8

2 4 6 8 10 9 7 5 3 1

Contents

CONTENTS

List of Maps and Illustrations

Acknowledgements

No book on an area as diverse and fascinating as Champagne can be written without the support and help of the growers and winemakers of the region. So, first of all, I should like to thank my numerous friends and acquaintances in Champagne for their help, information and advice, not to mention the many bottles shared in the pursuit of knowledge.

Invidious though it may seem, it would be impossible to thank every single person by name, but special thanks are due to:

Françoise Peretti and the Champagne Information Service, Nellie Pateras & George Atkinson, Richard Geoffroy, Christian de Billy, Laurence Ployez, Patricia Sliwa, Claude Fourmon & Charles Hawkins, Alain Seydoux, Bill Gunn, Ray Perks, François Roland-Billecart, Jean-Philippe Gardet, Jean-Claude Rouzaud, Evelyne Roques-Boizel, Bruno Paillard, Christian Bizot, Catherine Seydoux, Pascal Leclerc-Briant, Regis Barthélemy, Jennifer Mansuy, Carol Colbach, Danielle Brissaud, Pascal Olier, Dr Bertrand Robillard, Frederic Panaïotis and Laurent Champs.

Finally, I owe a great debt of gratitude to my editor, Julian Jeffs, who has been enormously encouraging, even when circumstances delayed production, and, secondly, to Colin Deane, who helped type the manuscript, made countless suggestions and researched some arcane angles. Without their help this would have been a poorer thing.

Introduction

From its very beginnings as a still wine, champagne has always had its admirers, from kings and emperors down to characters such as Surtees's Mr Radcliffe who favoured boot tops cleaned with a mixture of champagne and apricot jam – a somewhat curious use for a sublime drink. And nothing succeeds like success, as is proved by the number of sparkling wines today made all over the world.

Champagne is associated with everything that makes the heart lift – with happiness, love, good times, celebrations, friendship, good company, laughter, marriages and christenings. It is a drink for almost any occasion and, if all we are told is true, may even be drunk, not from a glass, but from a lady's slipper!

Contrary to popular belief, champagne is not one wine but many. It may be a light, crisp, *blanc de blancs*; it may be pink and foaming, or rich and weighty; it may be very dry or have distinct sweetness; the fizz may be aggressive or gentle; it may be a noble wine of great age, the colour of champagne silk and having an aroma of toasted hazelnuts. In short, you may buy champagne of whatever style you fancy, provided it has bubbles and is not red. It is a universal drink, shown off to perfection in long, narrow glasses with a column of small, steadily rising bubbles.

No wonder, then, that its praises have been sung in literature from Restoration times onwards. Mr Jorrocks in Paris may have observed that 'Champagne certainly gives one werry gentlemanly ideas', even if he did feel that he might prefer mild ale, but Hilaire Belloc understood its universal appeal. As he wrote *On a Great Election*:

> The accursed power which stands on Privilege
> (And goes with Women, and Champagne, and Bridge)

Broke – and Democracy resumed her reign:
(Which goes with Bridge, and Women, and Champagne).

For many years I have enjoyed drinking the wines of Champagne, and since my first visit have become more and more fascinated not only by the range of styles available from this unique method of production, but also by the history and the people themselves. Every visit brings new discoveries and, hopefully, a little more understanding. But in this fascination I am merely one among a multitude. Today, Champagne is easily reached from these shores, and every year a steady stream of visitors pours into Reims, Epernay, Aÿ, Cramant and the other great villages, coming to learn and to buy from their favourite producers. In this they are joined by champagne lovers from all over the world.

Yet, in some ways, I feel that champagne remains a misunderstood wine. Often those people professing the greatest love for the wines fail to realise how great these wines at their very best can be. Maybe this is due to the bubbles; perhaps there is a feeling that no wine with a fine mousse can possibly be the equal of a great burgundy or bordeaux. If so, this is not only a pity, it is also incorrect, for the greatest champagnes have an elegance, a depth and length of flavour second to none, and great complexity.

In writing this book, I have tried to share some of my fascination and joy in the region and its wine, and also to express my hopes for the future of this unique wine. Despite its glamour, neither the growers nor the makers have ever had a really easy time, and there is no doubt that today Champagne stands at a crossroads with some difficult choices to be made. We wish them good luck in the coming millennium.

Maggie McNie
Kent, 1998

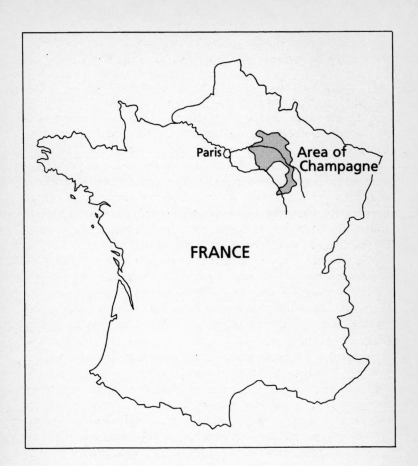

I
La Champagne

The wine-growing area known as la Champagne Viticole is situated about eighty-five miles north-east of Paris. Much of it lies in the valley of the Marne River, a tributary of the Seine – the means by which the wines were, in past centuries, transported to Paris where they were always popular. The district lies very far north, between 49 and 50° latitude, just on the edge of the climatic conditions which enable the vine to ripen its grapes, unless helped by specific mesoclimates as in Alsace, for example, or on the slopes of the Rhine.

The ancient capital of the province lies far to the south in Troyes, but today the wine-growing area has two main centres: the town of Epernay and the old city of Reims. It is a small area of about 35,000 hectares, or somewhat less than 100,000 acres, which lies mainly in the department of the Marne, with about 17 per cent of the vineyard area in the Aube, near Troyes, and the tiny remainder split between the departments of the Aisne and the Seine-et-Marne.

Being so far north, Champagne has a difficult climate. It is described, in wine-growing parlance, as northerly continental, but with a slight influence from the Atlantic Ocean. In simple terms, this means that it is highly marginal, with only just sufficient warmth to ripen the grapes, something which will happen only if the temperature averaged throughout the year is at least 10°C (50 °F); in other words, it has a very cool climate which in turn can mean a number of serious problems for the grapes.

First, the winters are occasionally cold enough to kill some vines. It takes intense cold for a few days to do this. If the temperature falls to minus 30°C, the sap will freeze in the vine, expanding and destroying the internal structure, at which point the plant turns black and simply rots. This happened in the winter of 1984/85 and Champagne lost one in ten of its vines. During late January and early February 1997 the temperature fell to −28 °C, and the vines were able to survive; a further drop of two degrees would have killed them.

It is an area that suffers from late frosts. These can damage and kill the young developing buds or shoots, and thereby the potential harvest for that year. Admittedly, these shoots will come again, but later. This almost certainly reduces the size of the crop, affecting the time of flowering and so the harvest, and some of the grapes may not have time to ripen. Indeed, in 1997 an early burst of warmth saw shoots well advanced by the Easter weekend, after which the temperature dropped considerably, initially stunting development, while later frosts cut the expected crop.

Conditions at flowering time are also vital. If the days are warm and without too much breeze, a good flowering and set can be expected; if damp and with fluctuating temperatures, the opposite can happen. In 1997, the early cold weather prevented flowering until July, which is late, and even then cold, damp conditions were less than perfect. In this particular vintage the uncertain start was made up for by a hot August and a completely dry September, when not a drop of rain fell during the harvest, something unheard of, but this cannot be relied upon, as both August and September are frequently damp.

One advantage of this cool climate, however, is that in most years the grapes get a long, slow ripening period which is a factor in the finished wine. The initial balance of acidity to ripeness and sugar is certainly not perfect for a still wine, but after the second fermentation – in which the bubbles are introduced into the wine – has been induced, it produces the hallmark delicacy and elegance of fine champagne. Often in very hot years, such as 1976, this balance vanishes because the speed of ripening upsets the all-important acid-to-sugar ratio, resulting in big, rich wines with low acidity.

The rolling hills of the district owe their existence to prehistoric earthquakes. Indeed, but for the resulting slopes, the entire region would not be able to harvest ripe grapes at all. To the south of Epernay lies the Côte des Blancs. At an altitude of about 180m (600ft) and stretching southwards for no more than 21km (13 miles), it finishes at Vertus with its beautiful twelfth-century church built over St Martin's Well. Facing it is Mont Aimé, famous (or infamous) for the execution in 1239 of the Cathars and also the site of a review by Tsar Alexander of 300,000 Prussian, Russian and Austrian troops in 1815.

The Montagne de Reims itself is only 19km (12 miles) long and covered on the plateau at its top by thick forests of deciduous trees, a great area for *la chasse*, shown in the autumn and winter by the sheer number of cars parked alongside the main Reims to Epernay road. Visitors to Reims are always advised to see the great Cathedral and the Palais de Tau, which now houses an exhibition devoted to the destruction wreaked by bombardment during the First World War. However no one should miss the older Basilica of St Rémi, now almost surrounded by a housing estate but an amazing and magnificent ninth-century church, within easy walking distance from the houses of Veuve Clicquot, Pommery or Taittinger. The Valley of the Marne, flowing westwards from Epernay, covers the area famous in the early days of champagne for producing the *vins de la rivière*. Today it has been extended as far as Dormans and Château-Thierry, although most of the villages here rate relatively low on the *échelle des crus* (the scale of quality given to the different vineyards). Seen from the road, which winds its way along the northern side of the Marne, it comprises wonderful rolling vineyards, almost a chocolate-box view of Champagne.

For the more adventurous there is a drive south to the Aube, with a collection of delightful villages. The mediaeval city of Troyes contains half-timbered buildings, stained glass and sculptures, while towards Arconville lies the forest of Clairvaux and the famous Cistercian abbey founded by St Bernard, which was used as a prison during the Revolution. Admirers of General de Gaulle can visit Colombey-les-deux-Eglises, and on the way see the great Cross of Lorraine memorial as well as his tomb in the tiny cemetery by the church.

The villages themselves are not spectacular, but are made up of solid yet elegant houses which often hide presses and wineries. Little signs show the way to small growers, where passing visitors are welcomed and shown the product of the house. Quite a high percentage of champagne sales are made directly from the cellar (or house) door.

One of the first impressions gained by the first-time visitor is the wonderful warmth and hospitality shown by the people of

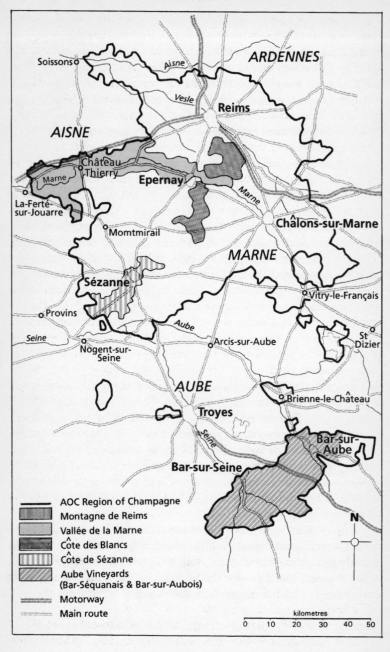

Soissons

Aisne

ARDENNES

Vesle

Reims

AISNE

Marne

Château
Thierry

Epernay

Marne

La-Ferté-
sur-Jouarre

Châlons-sur-Marne

Momtmirail

MARNE

Sézanne

Vitry-le-Français

Provins

Aube

St
Dizier

Seine

Nogent-sur-
Seine

Arcis-sur-Aube

AUBE

Brienne-le-Château

Troyes

Seine

Bar-sur-
Aube

Bar-sur-Seine

N

AOC Region of Champagne

Montagne de Reims

Vallée de la Marne

Côte des Blancs

Côte de Sézanne

Aube Vineyards
(Bar-Séquanais & Bar-sur-Aubois)

Motorway

Main route

kilometres

0   10   20   30   40   50

4

Champagne, perhaps tempered by a slight reserve until the realisation dawns that the guest is as enamoured of champagne as the host. 'I can see,' said one hostess happily, 'that you do not need a spittoon.' Another, at a time of serious shortage of the wine, referred to in wonderful English 'a parlous lack of liquid', which did not prevent several other bottles being opened. 'Would you like some tea?' asked yet another, producing a bottle of superb wine when answered in the affirmative. In good times and bad, visitors are always treated to the best that can be offered.

There is undoubtedly a close relationship here with serious visitors, rather than simply tourists, and in particular with the British. It was demonstrated, maybe, by the quiet but effective resistance of the Second World War, where all levels of society were involved in sabotage, from members of great merchant houses to the railway workers of Epernay, and all are remembered on the memorial in that town. The small house of Ployez Jacquemart in Ludes on the Montagne de Reims was home to certain RAF personnel during the phoney-war period, and no doubt at least one of the comments scratched on the walls, shown today with great pride to British visitors, had to be covered securely during the Occupation.

Champagne is also an area for the gourmet. It has a great food tradition, which for some curious reason is not as well known as that of, say, Provence, the Rhône, Périgord, Alsace or Burgundy. But it is well worth researching, even if the inevitable result is extra *avoirdupois*. There are superb salads; fish, including pike, salmon, eel, trout, carp and freshwater crayfish, is delicious, and often cooked in champagne sauces. Good beef and plenty of ham, veal and lamb, but most particularly rabbit, so long ignored across the Channel, but much appreciated in France, appear in many different guises. Game abounds, as might be expected in an area devoted to hunting. There are plenty of dishes based on pheasant, often marinated and cooked in red wine or in marc de champagne, and wild boar, wonderfully tasty and sometimes served with bilberries or sour cherries. Chicken appears in many forms, and then there is the great dish traditionally given to the pickers at harvest time: a stew of pork, ham, sausage with onions, carrots, cabbage, turnips and potatoes, both filling and delicious.

Cheese, too, plays a large part on the menu: Boursault, from the area where in 1845 a magnificent château was built for the Veuve Clicquot; the famous Brie de Meaux; tangy, rich Chaource and

Maroilles, whose origins lie in Flanders which is now very much a Champagne cheese. These are but a few of the culinary delights awaiting the visitor, in an area which boasts a number of Michelin-starred restaurants, including Gérard Boyer's famous Les Crayères.

2
Prehistory

Crossing the English Channel and driving to Champagne, one leaves behind the white cliffs of Dover and, on arriving at Calais, encounters relatively flat and uninspiring countryside which gradually starts to undulate. Finally, on the right-hand side, there is a slope crowned by the cathedral of the city of Laon and then, shortly ahead, further slopes which make up the Champagne vineyards.

The province of Champagne-Ardennes should not be confused with la Champagne Viticole, the wine-growing part. In absolute geological terms there are five distinctly different districts within the Champagne-Ardennes, but only one small part has developed the conditions in which the vine can bear and ripen fruit this far north.

La Champagne Viticole is part of an enormous chalk basin which stretches from the South Downs to the Montagne de Reims. It is centred on the Île-de-France and is known to the French as the Paris Basin, and, more generally, as the Franco-British Chalk Basin.

This entire geological area is the result of the retreat of a massive sea which took place some 70 million years ago. This sea had witnessed the development of various marine organisms, such as sea urchins, sponges and especially belemnites: a family of cephalopods with distinctive, bullet-shaped inner cells. The receding waters left huge deposits of these creatures in fossilised form, and a number of mineral deposits, not to mention some loamy-clay deposits. These were mainly left as great beds of chalk. La Champagne Viticole is the result of a series of geological accidents dating from the Tertiary Period.

The term 'chalk' is used very loosely by many writers, but chalk is in fact a specific form of limestone and the two terms are not interchangeable. A true chalk contains a high number of grains of

7

calcite that derive from marine life. It is excellent for the tap roots of vines as it is able both to hold moisture and, at the same time, to allow surplus water to drain away. On the debit side, it lacks a number of essential nutrients although these can always be added, and being so lime-rich makes it difficult for the vine to take essential minerals such as iron and copper from the soil, as any gardener of alkaline soil knows.

Two massive earthquakes during the Tertiary Period shook and twisted these great chalk deposits, which are in many instances 300m (1,000ft) deep, raising them to the levels that create the slopes of Champagne, known as the *falleuses*, and giving them a very thin deposit of important topsoil. These earthquakes created two distinct lines of hills – the Montagne de Reims and the hills to the south of Epernay – and what we call the Valley of the Marne.

There was a vast gap in time between the two earthquakes – the first taking place 30 million years ago. This centred on the Île-de-France, lifting the floor of the dried-up sea some 60m (200ft), twisting and breaking the soil, and pushing to the surface a mass of tertiary debris (chalk and mineral matter which helps to form the topsoil of Champagne). The enormously violent second earthquake, which took place 11 million years ago, raised the young hills to a much higher level – between 150-300m (500 to 1000ft) – again leaving behind a thin layer of similarly composed topsoil.

For generations it was believed that the elegance of the wines of Champagne could be attributed to this chalk, but a closer look at the soils suggests that the position is more complicated. These chalk beds, known as Campanian, are widely distributed throughout the Paris Basin. The characteristic fossils of the top layer are belemnites. At the lower level, the belemnites become rare and their place is taken by fossils of small sea urchins, micraster. Both forms are found in the Champagne vineyards, which are geographically delimited in a way that the Campanian chalk is not.

Dr Geoffrey Tresise, in a fascinating series of articles looking at the effects of geology on vine growing, suggests that a more likely reason is the mixture of the chalk and the lignite-rich deposits which form part of the thin layer of topsoil. He believes that lignite, a half-way stage between peat and coal, rich in carbon – itself an essential element for healthy plant growth – enriches the topsoil and that this unique combination, with the vine roots passing

8

through the topsoil and into the chalk, is a more likely reason for the restricted vineyard area.*

No one would deny the importance of these chalk beds. As well as keeping the roots dry, which is essential in a difficult climate, chalk also retains heat, thus assisting the ripening process. Last, but by no means least, the soft and easily excavated chalk has enabled a network of galleries to be dug underground producing the perfect conditions for the wine to develop.

First-time visitors to Champagne tend to expect the entire area shown as blocks on the viticultural map to be exactly that, and are often amazed to discover the woods, grazing land and other crops which also thrive there. The vineyard areas are mostly found scattered along the slopes of the hills. They are carefully positioned to avoid floods (in 1994, when the Marne burst its banks, the lowest-lying vineyards were only just above the floodwater line) and to minimize the risk of frost. Equally important, they must be low enough to be sheltered since in such a marginal climate correct exposure can be a vital element in the ripening process.

The autoroute into Reims from Calais reaches the city without passing through vineyards at all, and it is not until leaving on the main route south to Epernay that one enters vineyard country. Visitors approaching from Paris, whether by train or motorway, have a much earlier view as the Marne Valley vineyards come into sight just before Château-Thierry, while arriving by road from the Soissons direction, the route to Reims lies through the vineyards.

Traditionally, the greatest vineyards are held to be within three areas: the Montagne de Reims, from the commune of Villedom-mange through Verzy and surrounding villages, and finishing at Champillon, just outside Epernay; the Vallée de la Marne from Champillon westwards to Dormans and Château-Thierry; and the Côte des Blancs, southwards from Epernay and finishing at Ber-gères-lès-Vertus.

On the Montagne, the all-important subsoil tends to be the belemnitic chalk on the higher slopes, with micraster on the lower, as would be expected. The Côte des Blancs is also mainly belemnitic chalk, but of considerably less depth in places where it begins to turn sandy, and some micraster on the lower slopes, while the

* Dr. Geoffrey Tresise, Keeper of Geology, Merseyside County Museum, Liverpool, in a series of articles on Wine and Geology for the magazine *Wine & Spirit*.

Vallée de la Marne also has belemnitic chalk which rises above the lower-lying river soils on which no vines are planted. Further west in the valley, the chalk lessens, and gravel, clay, marl and sandstone are all found. Indeed, looking over the vineyards in the Marne Valley, there is visibly less chalk here than in other parts.

Topsoils are much more complex. The Montagne has considerable chalk rubble, with some sand, lignite and 'head' – a curious term, in French called *colluvium*. In essence, head is a deposit left following the Pleistocene glaciation. During the thaw, this material slid down from higher ground and is highly fertile. Professor J. M. Hancock of Imperial College, London believes that head is an important part of the Champagne topsoil.

The warm topsoils found in the Côte des Blancs are a mixture of clay, lignite and sand, although some flint does appear around Vertus, while the Marne Valley contains marl, usually described as a mixture of clay and limestone (although its composition varies from almost entirely clay to almost entirely limestone, lignite and sandstone).

Two other areas need to be considered. South-west of Epernay lies the Côte de Sézanne, where the subsoil comprises mainly chalk of both varieties, with topsoils including sandstone, marl, and clay. Lignite is also found, not only in the topsoil but also in deposits sufficient to allow mining.

The one Champagne district with a very different soil structure is the Aube. It should be remembered that the commune of Les Richeys, which is incidentally the largest, is 160km (100 miles) further south, near Troyes, the old capital of Champagne, and only about 64km (40 miles) from Chablis. And just like Chablis, the subsoil is mostly of Kimmeridgian clay. The topsoil is gravelly limestone, with a high proportion of stones which retain heat and assist with ripening. Because of this, and as the vineyards are, in the main, planted on steep south-facing slopes, the Aube vineyards have proved highly suitable for growing Pinot Noir.

3

Lords of the Vineyards of Aÿ

'We are specialists in war and white wine', wrote a distinguished winemaker from Alsace. The same statement is true of Champagne. A brief look at the map shows the situation only too clearly.

The Champagne region lies at the crossroads. Any invader from the north seeking passage to the warmer south will almost certainly march through the area, as its history from the armies of Attila to the battles of the First World War bears witness. It is truly amazing that this countryside not only made wines at all, but also that those wines, at least from the ninth century, appear to have been highly appreciated.

It is impossible to be certain when the first vines were cultivated here. Much has been made of the discovery during the nineteenth century of some fossilised vine leaves embedded in tertiary chalk. However, *vitis sesannensis*, as the vine was named, seems to have been a wild species unsuitable for winemaking, and although no serious date can be given for the start of winemaking anywhere, let alone in Champagne, the notion of prehistoric man making wine is untenable in the light of current knowledge. In any case, although the oldest vineyards in France are believed to be in Provence, planted either by Phocaean Greeks fleeing the heavy hand of Cyrus II, or slightly earlier by the Phoenicians around 600 BC, there is no real evidence to suggest that winemaking spread any further north than Vienne until the middle of the first century AD.

That the Gauls were very fond of drinking wine is clear from Roman sources. It appears that slaves were traded for wine, but although Columella, writing at the start of the first century, mentions vines being grown in Gaul, it is equally apparent from archaeological excavations at burial sites that trade in wine services and storage vessels from the Mediterranean – and therefore, by

11

inference, wine itself – had been taking place centuries before the arrival of the Romans. Nevertheless, as in many other areas, the catalyst here was the influence of their all-conquering legions. Julius Caesar, that great observer of the lands he subjugated, certainly failed to mention the existence of vineyards in Champagne, but today it is generally agreed that the Romans introduced viticulture to Burgundy around the middle of the first century, and that three other areas were developed shortly afterwards: Champagne, Alsace and Bordeaux.

The forested state of much of the area must have made the process slow, and anyway seems to have been halted by the edict of the Emperor Domitian in AD 92 prohibiting further plantings of vines and even ordering the uprooting of many outside Italy. But following the repeal of this law by Probus (naturally known as the Wine Emperor) in AD 282, the grateful inhabitants of Champagne once more began to develop their vineyards and enjoy a stable and prosperous existence. The days of peace, however, were destined to be short-lived, for already the Roman Empire was under attack from the migrating barbarian tribes, notably the Franks, Alamans, Goths, Visigoths and Vandals. Although the early probing and looting raids were easily defeated, the Gallo-Roman city of Durocortorum (later Reims) was first burnt to the ground in 355 by a raiding party from across the Rhine, and destroyed again in 406. But the greatest threat was yet to come: invasion by the hordes of Attila the Hun.

The 'Scourge of God' swept down on the Empire from the east, leading an army said to number over 500,000 men. The Huns were believed both to eat and sleep in the saddle when on the march, and every enemy fell before them. Their cruelty was legendary, as were the stories of the feasts and drunken debauchery which followed their victorious advances. In the spring of 451, Attila crossed the Rhine and descended on Gaul, reaching the Champagne region in May. Here, at last, his advance was checked. Reims was razed yet again, and after a two-month siege Orléans fell, but by now a Roman army had found him. It was led by Aëtius, and contingents from two of Rome's barbarian adversaries, the Visigoths and the Franks, were marching with him.

On 21 September the two armies met on the plain near Châlons-sur-Marne. The great battle lasted into the next day, at the end of which Aëtius was victorious. According to contemporary records,

200,000 men perished. Rather than pursuing and destroying the remnants of the Hunnish horde, Aëtius besieged Attila in his fortified encampment but finally gave the Huns safe passage back across the Rhine. The respite for Champagne, however, was brief. The Roman victory had been achieved only at the expense of alliance with other invading enemies against the common foe. The Roman Empire in the west was fading fast. Less than fifty years after the defeat of Attila most of Gaul had fallen to the Franks, led by their very able king, Clovis.

According to tradition, Clovis and 3,000 of his followers were baptised on Christmas Day 496 by St Rémi. Two factors appear to have influenced this mass conversion: the stalwart and unceasing missionary efforts of St Rémi himself and the the influence of Clovis's Christian wife-to-be, a princess of the Burgundians named Clothilde. Faced with a devastating defeat in battle, Clovis is said to have called on God in despair, whereupon the tide immediately turned in his favour.

Whatever the truth of the matter, the conversion of Clovis was of enormous significance. The Church had established its influence with the new rulers of Gaul, and the victories of Clovis over his main rivals – the Visigoths in the south and the Burgundians to the east – effectively created the Kingdom of France, stretching from the Mediterranean Sea to the English Channel. In his gratitude, Clovis heaped favours on the city of St Rémi in whose cathedral generations of Kings of France would be crowned. Of even greater importance for the future of the region's wines, the establishment of Christianity as the religion of the Franks led to the foundation of many monasteries. The Benedictines founded no fewer than six in the diocese of Reims alone – all of them with vineyards.

The vital contribution made by the monastic movement to the development of wine is rarely appreciated. The monks largely saved the art of viticulture as the Roman Empire disintegrated and they kept the light of culture and viticulture burning throughout the Dark Ages, in spite of constant invasions occasioning looting and the destruction of buildings and cities. There is no doubt about the importance of wine to the monks. They needed it to celebrate Mass, to drink themselves, to offer to travellers who rested overnight in their guest houses, and to sell, for the upkeep of a large monastic establishment was considerable.

The first references to the wines of Champagne date back to the ninth century, divided into wines of the river and wines of the mountains, but the real growth in reputation came during the tenth to thirteenth centuries. This was a relatively peaceful and stable period – except for the fierce struggle for the French throne during which Hugh Capet burnt Epernay in 947 and removed all available wine. Hugh's son, another Hugh, was eventually crowned King of France in Reims in 987.

Just as Champagne stood at a crossroads for invading armies, so it was also well situated for trade between the northern countries and those from the warmer south, and the establishment of regular trade fairs spread the fame of the Champagne wines. They took place throughout the region and each was held annually, starting with the January Fair in Lagny and finishing with the October Fair in Troyes. Each could last as long as forty-nine days. There were six in all, so trading would have taken place almost continuously. These were mainly cloth or textile fairs where goods from Flanders and the north were traded for silks and spices, for example, brought up from the Mediterranean, where the Genoese and Venetians had well-established trade contacts with the Orient. With so many merchants regularly visiting the region, the wine's fame began to spread, helped also by the election in 1088 of Pope Urban II from Champagne, who made no secret of his predilection for the wines of his homeland. Eventually wine merchants from other countries began to visit the Champagne Fairs, but by the end of the thirteenth century the growth in maritime trade had moved the emphasis from the landlocked north to the Straits of Gibraltar and the fairs died out.

During this period there are indications of an increasing sophistication in perception of the wines. Specific areas or *crus* came to the fore, those of Aÿ, Epernay, and Mailly being specially recommended. Fighting, however, returned to the area with the outbreak of the Hundred Years War in 1337 and once again Champagne became a principal battlefield among the forces of France, England and, from 1417, Burgundy. The population appears to have been devastated by war and plague, with survivors retreating to the caves on the Montagne de Reims and the Côtes des Blancs. Although the vineyards must necessarily have been neglected, winemaking did continue; the appointment of professional wine brokers, the *courtiers en vin*, had occurred by 1323, and a royal charter dated July

1412 provides clear evidence that wine was regarded as the principal business in Reims.

In spite of the victory of the English at Agincourt and the recognition by the mad King Charles VI of Henry V as his heir, the resurgence of the French cause was imminent. In 1429, inspired by the determination of Joan of Arc, the French crowned the Dauphin as Charles VII in the cathedral at Reims. And it is worth noting that present in his capacity as a municipal magistrate was a M. Moët.* Champagne was effectively in French hands once more.

Following the expulsion of the English, the vineyards appear to have flourished and the growing reputation of the wine (not to mention the price paid for it), suggests that there had been a good deal of improvement in quality during the fifteenth century. Earlier in its history the Champagne wine seems to have been regarded as rather strong, since special mention was made of those with the temerity to drink it undiluted. Given the cool northerly climate of the region, which would give natural light levels of alcohol, Patrick Forbes has raised the possibility that the wine might have been strengthened with some form of crude distillate from further south. It is unlikely that the truth will ever be known, but Thibaut IV of Champagne excused his drinking of the wine neat on account of his 'cold stomach', while the Holy Roman Emperor Wenceslaus of Bohemia, while on an official visit to Reims in 1397, became so drunk on this rough, strong wine that he was unable to transact his business. It is only fair to add, however, that this appears to have been something of a regular occurrence with His Majesty.

Despite the general popularity of the Champagne wines by the fifteenth century, one area stands out as being the most sought-after: Aÿ. Popes, Kings and Emperors either owned vineyards around Aÿ, or at least appointed agents to secure their supplies. Such was its prestige that it received a near accolade from a royal source. Henri IV, a great lover of both wine and women, and bored by the Spanish Ambassador's habit of announcing in full all the titles borne by His Most Catholic Majesty, is said to have replied

* The origin of the name Moët is uncertain, but the city annals record that Reims had magistrates of that name by the fifteenth century. Certainly one attended the coronation of Charles VII in 1429, and a member of the family was ennobled in 1446.

15

on one such occasion by styling himself simply as 'Henri, Lord of Aÿ'.

The Fronde – a bitter civil war fought between the adherents and adversaries of Cardinal Mazarin during the minority of Louis XIV – once again brought fighting to the Champagne vineyards, but the coronation of the young king ushered in a great period. Louis is said to have been delighted by the local wines offered him at his coronation, and he enjoyed and drank them for most of his life, thereby ensuring that the court and all smart society did likewise. And the wines were easily transported by boat up the Marne, into the Seine and so into Paris. His taste in this was matched, aided and abetted by a number of noblemen, one of whom, the Marquis de Saint-Evremonde, subsequently removed himself to London in order to avoid the King's displeasure which might well have left him immured in the Bastille for many years. M. de Saint-Evremonde introduced the English to the joys of the Champagne wines with far-reaching effects.

These still wines from Champagne were seriously rivalled only by wines from one other region: Burgundy. This rivalry lasted for almost two centuries. Certainly, Louis XIV from the time of his coronation took a particular liking to the red wines of Bouzy (according to the memoirs of Saint-Simon), leading to great prosperity for the region. This indulgence, however, was brought to an end in 1693 by the King's physician, Dr Fagon, when he prescribed burgundy rather than champagne for medical reasons. Doctors from the faculties of Beaune and Reims argued at length about the relative health-giving properties of their wines, but champagne was to change course and the rivalry died out.

Until the very end of the 1600s these popular early wines of Champagne were still wines made mostly from red grapes. It is clear from contemporary sources that they were of variable colour, bearing little resemblance to the modern conception of a red wine; probably something more approaching a *vin gris* or the rather nicely named *œil de perdrix* (partridge eye). The climate in Champagne is hardly conducive to producing high colouring matter in the skins except in the occasional very hot summer, and we know that the close of the seventeenth century saw some harsh climatic conditions.

In addition, there was a little wine made from white grapes only which was also highly sought after and recommended for its particular health-giving properties. One other oddity was recorded about these still wines. In the spring following the vintage, a slight sparkle was observed in them, presumably because the cold winters then prevailing had inhibited the yeast's action before the primary fermentation was complete or any malolactic or secondary fermentation had taken place.* The process simply restarted as the temperatures rose during the spring, but, of course, such knowledge was not available to seventeenth-century winemakers. They merely observed it, and nicknamed the wines *vins du diable*.

It was to take an enquiring and original mind to seek to harness this tendency of the wine to sparkle. And such a mind was close at hand, for not many years after the coronation of Louis XIV a young monk was appointed cellarer at the Abbey of Hautvillers. His name was Dom Pierre Pérignon, and under his care the wine of Champagne was to begin its evolution from a still *vin gris* into the sparkling wine that we know today.

---

* For a detailed description of this process, see pp. 72–3 or the Glossary.

4
Seeing Stars

From the first undoubtedly crude wine which developed somewhere between 1660 and 1690, it was to be an evolution of about 150 years before the sparkling wines of Champagne were finally accepted. As has already been noted, the vines of this cool northerly region with its very chalky soil had a natural tendency to effervesce, particularly in the rising temperatures of the spring months following the vintage. This may have been due to a resumption of the primary or alcoholic fermentation, interrupted by winter cold, or simply to the spontaneous start of the malolactic fermentation.

It is also worth remembering that, at this time, red grapes were thought to produce 'serious' wine, while white ones were far less well regarded. Also the red grapes were harvested earlier since it was believed that to pick them in the heat of the late summer would increase the amount of colour in the resulting wine. The 'lesser' white grapes were usually harvested much later, sometimes around All Saints Day,* and it was these which appear to have been used for the first sparkling wines. Today, of course, the practice is exactly the opposite, as grapes for dry white wines are universally picked first. However, winemakers of this period had no real scientific basis on which to work (after all, it was to be nearly 200 years before Louis Pasteur would publish his *Etudes sur les vins et les vinaigres* and explain the vinification process), merely a practical knowledge based upon observation and local traditions. Late picking of the white grapes lends itself to the theory that cold winter conditions inhibited the alcoholic fermentation process which would resume the following spring. This may well have been exacerbated by one of the greatest achievements of Dom Pérignon:

* See *The Story of Champagne*, Nicholas Faith, London, 1988.

the production of truly white wines from red grapes. He clearly understood that it was necessary to prevent colour seepage at the time of pressing and his highly specific instructions to the pickers – to harvest the grapes in cool conditions – were in direct contrast to customary practice. This may well have led to the harvesting of slightly under-ripe grapes with high acidity, which could well have contributed to the subsequent sparkle.

This effervescence was regarded as a fault in wine, and therefore a major problem which had to be addressed. Froth belonged to beer, or very possibly to drinking chocolate; in wine it was at the very least vulgar! Three and a half centuries later, sparkling wine is perceived to be very special, the wine of celebration, laughter and fun. So how, from these highly dubious origins and with all social pressures ranged against it, did sparkling wine evolve into one of the great classic wines of the world?

It is now perhaps worth asking why, in this second half of the seventeenth century, sparkling wine evolved at all. If this mousse in the wine was seen as a fault, there were two options for wine-makers: elimination (which was impossible given the then level of technical knowledge), or its control and development.

The idea of sparkling wine was not new. The Romans had noted the possibility and the Bible mentions 'wine that moveth'. Moreover, there is documentary evidence that the monks of the Abbey of St-Hilaire in Limoux had accepted orders for sparkling wine as early as 1531, a good 150 years before. Yet it is generally accepted that the origins of today's sparkling wines lie in the late seventeenth century and in Champagne.

As with so many discoveries and developments, the right conditions seemed to coincide at this period: essentially the stronger glass bottle and an airtight cork closure. Plainly no fully sparkling wine could be produced in barrel. To trap carbon dioxide in wine, it had to be kept completely closed against the air. Until the late seventeenth century, wine had never been sold in bottle, as we understand it today, but from the cask. Bottles were owned by individuals who took these fragile glass containers to the wine merchant. They were filled, and a stopper, normally an oil-soaked rag surrounded with twine, was placed in the neck. Occasionally, a thin wooden sliver was placed in the rag, but only if the wine, or the customer, was very special. Obviously no such storage arrangement could have preserved any serious foam in the wine.

And both requirements had to be present. Delicate glass with an airtight stopper would break under the pressure, while strong glass without an airtight closure would be wasted. Both these needs were about to be met; but this is why the sparkling wine orders placed at the Abbey of St-Hilaire would not have borne any resemblance to the wine that was about to develop in Champagne.

In 1615 King James I, urged on by Sir Robert Mansell, an Admiral of the Fleet, outlawed the increasing use of wood in glass furnaces, the Admiral and Parliament fearing the loss of the oak needed for shipbuilding. The resulting use of sea coal in the furnaces produced higher temperatures and therefore stronger glass. There is no firm evidence to show how or when news of this *verre anglais* reached Champagne, but it seems logical to suggest that the problems created in attempting to control the mousse prompted the makers to search for answers.

There is, however, another intriguing possibility: that sparkling wine was an accidental discovery which spread from England back to Champagne, where it was to be fully developed. This theory is rather more than a flight of fancy, since although the French traditionally and by law used casks for the storage and transport of wine, the English appeared to have bottled the lighter wines imported from the northern regions on their arrival in order to lengthen their lifespan. Moreover, they added 'vast quantities of sugar molasses ... to make them drink brisk and sparkling' according to a Dr Merret, writing in 1662.* This would explain the fact that by 1676 Sir George Etheredge, in his play *The Man of Mode*, was able to mention sparkling champagne.

The wines of Champagne seem to have been introduced into England through the influence of one member of a fellowship called the Ordre des Coteaux. This 'order of the slopes' consisted of a number of noblemen whose love of good food and wine was notorious. The name was bestowed upon them as a joke, following an incident where three of them had dined with the Bishop of Le Mans and astonished him by their extreme choosiness. According to Nicholas Faith, their 'veal had to come only from Normandy, their partridges from the Auvergne, and as for their wine, it had

---

* Refers to a paper read by Dr Merret to the newly formed Royal Society and entitled 'Observations'.

to come only from three particularly favoured slopes, Aÿ, Hautvillers and Epernay'.

One member of this Ordre des Coteaux was the Marquis de Saint-Evremonde, mentioned in the previous chapter. By 1661–2 he had offended Louis XIV to such a degree that he was banished for life, and he fled to London. Here he was befriended by King Charles II who gave him the wardenship of the tiny Duck Island in the lake in St James's Park. He was a most influential figure and undoubtedly introduced the wines of Champagne to the beau monde of Restoration London, and initiated the export trade between Champagne and England which continues strongly today. It was these wines which may have given rise to the first sparkling champagne.

The notion that sparkling wine was an English 'accidental discovery' is a delightful but immaterial idea, even if true. The climate in England at the time was far too cold for wine-growing, and to Champagne must go the honour of developing fully sparkling wine by a method which has taken three centuries to evolve, and indeed is still doing so.

The advent of the *verre anglais*, which was certainly being manufactured in France well before Dom Pérignon's death, and the discovery of cork for closures, meant that wines with a deliberately created mousse had become a possibility. There is a legend, one of many that will be discussed when assessing the true achievements of Dom Pérignon, which tells of the arrival at Hautvillers of two Spanish monks on their travels (monasteries were the hostels of their day). It is said that the water-skins they carried were stoppered with cork bark, and that on hearing about its miraculous properties, Pierre Pérignon immediately ordered a consignment. It was in his lifetime that cork came to be used, and that is what matters.

The first sparkling champagne is traditionally dated at 1690 when, again according to the legend of Dom Pérignon, he was heard calling to his brethren from the cellars under the abbey: 'Brothers, brothers come quickly for I am seeing stars!' These first sparkling wines were made by bottling the wine before the end of the alcoholic fermentation, thus trapping some carbon dioxide but also leaving sediment in the bottle. The resulting wine would have been cloudy and, certainly by today's standards, of relatively low pressure. This method existed until fairly recently and its nearest modern approximation can be seen in the Blanquette de Limoux Méthode Ancestrale AC.

We now know that the general practice was to store these bottles upside-down with their necks in sand, to drive as much of the sediment as possible on to the cork, and it seems that a crude form of *dégorgement à la volée* took place before the wine was served, decanting from one bottle into another, thereby reducing the effervescence. Strangely enough, it was to be almost 150 years before the next stage in the development of the method took place. The nineteenth century was to witness enormous technical advances, but the eighteenth attended to the gradual acceptance of a wine described in 1711 as '*cette abominable boisson*' and to the foundation of the trade in sparkling champagne in contrast to the still red wines which had been made previously.

5

The Main Claimants

Driving from Reims to Epernay, whether on the main road or the *route touristique*, looking to the right across one of the most famous views of the Champagne vineyards, there appears a spire; in the winter, with no leaves on the trees, the whole building is visible. During the summer months, the narrow streets around this landmark are crammed with visitors, for this is the abbey church of Hautvillers. In the nave lies a black marble flagstone with its Latin epitaph, marking the last resting place of Dom Pierre Pérignon. Many know the legend, but what are the facts of his story?

Pierre Pérignon was born in the village of Ste-Menehould either late in 1638 or very early in 1639, as his baptism is registered in the municipal archives as having taken place on 5 January 1639. He was born into a professional family, his father being registered as a judge's clerk. Most of the male members of the family appear to have been lawyers, but a fair number chose the Church. The next verifiable date in his life is 3 July 1658 when, aged only nineteen, he entered the Abbey of St-Vannes in Verdun.

This particular congregation had been founded by a Dom Didier de la Cour, who died in 1623, but who demanded high standards of intellectual ability, and by the time the young Pierre Pérignon entered the abbey its reputation had grown immensely. Although there are no records of his life between baptism and entry, the latter suggests that he had attained a high degree of learning and was showing considerable academic promise. Some years later (some records give 1668 and others 1670), aged thirty, at the most, he was sent to the Abbey of Hautvillers where he was appointed cellarmaster.

Cellarmaster, or cellarer, was a very senior appointment, second only in importance to that abbot. In today's terms Dom Pérignon could be regarded as chief executive. He was not only expected to take responsibility for the abbey's vineyards and winemaking, but also the sale of that wine, any building maintenance, the distribution of charity, the purchase of all provisions and other necessities, and the abbey's finances. That these onerous tasks were entrusted to a relatively young man sheds considerable light on his abilities. According to his epitaph, he carried out his duties meticulously for forty-seven years until his death in 1715 at the age of seventy-seven. Such, in brief, are the hard facts known about this man.

It is necessary, therefore, to investigate, or to read between the lines. A contemporary account of the Champagne vineyards considered the very best at the start of the eighteenth century lists them as: Sillery, Verzenay, Aÿ, Hautvillers, Pérignon and St-Thierry. And in his lifetime there is considerable evidence that 'les vins de Pérignon' commanded a heavy price premium.

Patrick Forbes mentions a letter dated 10 November 1700 from a winemaker, but also a merchant, based in Epernay to a M. d'Artagnan, who was a lieutenant-general in the army: 'Where an ordinary wine of Champagne cost 200 livres the queue, and a better one somewhere between 400 and 500 livres, wines from Hautvillers would fetch up to 900 livres.' This same winemaker, Bertin de Rocheret (son of the Sieur de Rocheret, who owned vineyards at Aÿ), also received letters from other customers requesting a supply of the Hautvillers wine, for, as M. d'Artagnan wrote in 1715, 'frankly, they are the best'. And if more evidence for the pre-eminence of these wines were needed, look to the words of Dom Pérignon's immediate successor as cellarmaster, Brother Pierre: 'the reverend Father Pérignon achieved the glory of giving the wines of Hautvillers the high reputation they enjoy from Pole to Pole' – undoubtedly an exaggeration, but one which shows the importance attached to these particular wines.

In examining the legend, it must first be stated that all evidence is either deduced or, at best, secondhand. In 1790, during the French Revolution, the monks finally fled the abbey and at that time all Dom Pérignon's papers disappeared. Still in existence, however, is a small treatise written by Brother Pierre on the culture of the vines in Champagne. This clearly documents the principles used by Dom Pérignon, who undertook many tasks which were regarded by most other vine growers to be either unnecessary or even impossible. He must have been a considerable innovator.

Until Dom Pérignon's time, the wines produced in the region were, on the whole, what would now be regarded as *vin gris*, not truly white. Most of the grapes then being grown were red varieties, but truly red wine had eluded the makers. According to Brother Pierre, by selecting the very ripest grapes from the very oldest vines, Dom Pérignon produced a genuinely red wine, but, most importantly, only in about four years out of ten when there was an unusually warm summer. Then, as now, the cool, northerly climate made it impossible in most vintages to ripen the red grapes sufficiently for strong colour pigmentation to be present in the skins.

Of more relevance to the development of the sparkling wine drunk today is that Dom Pérignon seems to have been the first to produce a truly white wine from these red grapes. His reputation in this matter was unassailable, not only in his time but also considerably later. On 25 October 1821, the last cellarmaster of the abbey, Dom Grossard, wrote to the deputy mayor of Aÿ, stating that it was Dom Pérignon who had 'discovered the secret of making . . . still white wine', adding that beforehand it had been the colour of grey or straw. Dom Grossard did not specify whether this technique was for red grapes, but since it is known that these were the majority of grapes then grown, it must follow that Dom Pérignon must have altered or amended in some way the manner of pressing them. Today at the Abbey of Hautvillers it is possible to see a very old wine press, a much cruder version of the classical Champagne press still used, dating from approximately Dom Pérignon's time. Its use allowed for a swift pressing of the grapes, thus producing a clear white juice: a miracle in those days.

Another innovation which owes it existence to Dom Pérignon appears to be the idea of blending wines from different vineyard areas in the region, as he understood that the sum of parts would be greater than the individual. No doubt this idea was not completely new, but it does seem that Dom Pérignon was the first to grasp the fact that the final *cuvée* gave the quality to the finished wine. According to Brother Pierre, although Dom Pérignon did not taste the grapes in the vineyards, he did regularly inspect them as they approached maturity, and would arrange for sample grapes to be delivered to him at the end of each day's picking, after which he would leave the samples on his window ledge until the following morning. On tasting, which was always before breakfast, he would make his blends, 'not only according to the flavour of the juice, but also according to what the weather had been like that year – an early or late development, depending on the amount of cold or rain there had been – and according to whether the vines had grown a rich or mediocre foliage'.

Today we are used to the fragmentation of the Champagne vineyards, but it is important to remember that this break-up was one consequence of the French Revolution. In the late seventeenth century, the Abbey of Hautvillers had very large vineyard holdings. According to Patrick Forbes, in 1636 it owned some 100 arpents of land (an arpent is roughly equivalent to an acre) or 40 hectares. Almost certainly this would have increased by Dom Pérignon's time, the faithful often leaving land to an abbey in return for their prayers, and they would also have derived grapes from the tithe system. There would have been grapes from many different areas available to the winemaker.

Another factor would undoubtedly have been, at least towards the end of his life, Dom Pérignon's total blindness. As so often happens, when one sense is lost another appears to develop extra sensitivity. Dom Grossard wrote, 'He could tell at once, without being told, which grapes came from which vineyard, and he would say, "The wine of that vineyard must be married with the wine of that one," and never did he make a mistake.'

We have seen how neither the fragile glass nor the makeshift stoppers of the day were suitable for containing a sparkling wine, but while Dom Pérignon and others in the region were experimenting, these problems were being solved.

It is not known how cork arrived in the region. One story suggests that, as a very young man, Dom Pérignon travelled to Alcántara in Spain. This is not an impossibility, but there is no real evidence to support this theory, certainly not in Spain itself, although Patrick Forbes does mention a local tradition in Estremadura that he did spend time there working in the cork forests.

The second, and possibly better known, legend concerns the pilgrim monks from Santiago de Compostela's overnight stay at Hautvillers. Their water bottles were sealed with a spongy material which had kept the water fresh, and this so intrigued the curious Dom Pérignon that he requested supplies. It is unlikely that we shall ever know the truth, but another piece of the jigsaw was in place, and it is reasonably certain that this is also to the credit of the cellarmaster of Hautvillers.

Good clear white juice from red grapes, the *cuvée* and the arrival of cork were three major factors in the development of sparkling champagne, but the last, vital element concerned the fragile bottles. Whether before, or during, Dom Pérignon's tenure as cellarmaster at Hautvillers the stronger *verre anglais* began to be manufactured in France remains a matter for conjecture, but by that time the technique was known in France. There is a record of the '*verrières de Sainte-Menehould*', originally established by M. Colbert, the Finance Minister to Louis XIV and himself born in Reims, to create employment in districts of low standards of living. Is it beyond the bounds of possibility that learning of a cellarmaster born in Ste-Menehould Colbert patronised a glass works connected with the village?

In any event, by the date given for production of the first sparkling champagne in 1690 all the elements were in place. In 1718, the treatise of Brother Pierre was published. In it he states that the 'French took to sparkling champagne more than 20 years ago', which just about agrees. He also remarked that the French 'developed a positive mania for it', a fact rather more dubious considering its early '*abominable*' reputation.

The question, however, remains: was sparkling champagne first created by Dom Pérignon? Unless his personal papers ever come to light, and this is now highly unlikely, there will never be a definitive answer. His reputation truly rests on other factors, without which the wine we know today would not have developed. That he was a great winemaker is beyond doubt, but there were other highly gifted people working in Champagne at the same time who also have a stake in the sparkling-wine legend. Pre-eminent among these is Frère Jean Oudart.

In his *History of Champagne*, Henry Vizetelly mentions Jean Oudart as another monk with a claim to fame in the early history of sparkling champagne, and at least one major house, Taittinger, champions his cause. In 1680, according to Claude Taittinger in his very interesting book *Champagne*, Jean Oudart, a lay brother originally from Dormans, was placed in charge of the estate in Pierry, at that time the property of the Benedictine abbey of St Peter-on-the-Mount in Châlons.

Frère Oudart was considerably younger than Dom Pérignon and soon gained an outstanding reputation not only for viticulture, but also for the quality of the wines he produced. These were frequently handled by the same merchant, Bertin de Rocheret, as were those of Hautvillers, and history records at least one meeting between Dom Pérignon and Frère Oudart at Pierry on 9 September 1713. But in the manner of winemakers, wherever they are based, it would be likely that they also corresponded and discussed problems on other occasions. Certainly in these early experimental days, when results must often have been somewhat disappointing, Jean Oudart's success was such that other monks were sent from Benedictine abbeys to learn from him.

Little else is documented concerning this Brother, with one exception. The parish registers kept at the Town Hall showed that he had died in early May 1742 and had been buried, on the 12th, in the nave of the church as befitted such an eminent person. One other fact was known about him, namely that he was of a great height for that period: just short of six feet. Armed with such information the search for his body began in the spring of 1972 under the auspices of the house of Taittinger which had promised to re-lay the nave, then showing signs of considerable wear and tear. On 17 April the search reached its climax with the discovery of Frère Oudart's tomb. Measurement of the blackened bones confirmed the stories of his great stature, and in addition his jaw bone, of a man of 87 years at his death, held seventeen good teeth.

After a number of days for the local inhabitants to inspect and to meditate on these relics, the remains of Frère Oudart were given burial in the presence of many local dignitaries and representatives from the champagne industry. A marble plaque recalling his achievements can now be seen in the church at Pierry, and should be included on the *route touristique* for all lovers of Champagne. They will also notice that the village hall and a street bear his name.

6

The Evolution of the Method

By 1690, what the master winemakers of the region were producing, in effect, was a white wine with some carbonic acid gas trapped within it, which had become possible owing to the stronger glass, and cork closures tied down with string. But the wine was cloudy and probably in pressure terms little more than faintly sparkling (*pétillant*) but considerably less effervescent than modern sparkling wines. This novelty was sold alongside the still wines of the region, and it is unlikely that any long-term future for it was foreseen. Bertin de Rocheret (from whose letters much of the early developments of the champagne trade can be gleaned) strongly advised against adding sparkle to any fine wine, believing that such treatment should be reserved for lesser wines only, 'and rightly belongs to beer, chocolate and whipped cream', thus putting the new wine firmly in its place.

However, another factor may well help to explain the slow acceptance of this newfangled drink: historically, the timing was unpropitious. The long reign of the Sun King was drawing to its end. Louis XIV and his mistress, later morganatic wife, the highly religious convert from the Huguenot faith to Roman Catholicism, Mme de Maintenon, presided over the court at Versailles. Piety, not parties, was the order of the day – hardly the best time to launch the new foaming wine, which was bound to be perceived as frivolous.

Thus it was not until after Louis' death in 1715, and the accession of the young Louis XV under the regency of the Duc d'Orléans, that sparkling champagne began to show its long-term potential. The Regent occupied the Palais Royal, soon the centre of a highly frivolous and extravagant beau monde, and it was here that the new sparkling style received the seal of approval. Indeed the Regent's mother, a princess of Bavaria, wrote as early as August 1716: 'When my son gets tipsy it is not on strong drinks or spiritous [*sic*] liquors, but on the pure wine of Champagne.' By the middle of the century, so well established had it become at court that Mme de Pompadour gave champagne her famous endorsement. 'Champagne,' she said, 'is the only wine that leaves a woman beautiful after drinking it.' Failure thereafter was never a possibility.

Most of the developments which changed this sparkling wine into the drink we know today came in the nineteenth century, but one important innovation came about during the reign of Louis XV. The new wine depended for its sparkle on being made and sold in the bottle, but French law specified the transportation of wine in cask only. There is little doubt that greater nobility and the extremely wealthy managed to evade the law and obtain their champagne in bottles, but the majority wishing to sample this novelty had to purchase it from the cask, thus losing almost all the effervescence. This seriously hampered the emerging trade.

In 1724, a petition was submitted to Louis, now reigning in person, requesting him to amend the law in this one instance. The demand for sparkling champagne was increasing strongly as customers showed their preference for this style. It took the King about four years to be convinced by their arguments, which were presumably opposed by his Treasury ministers as the reason for the original law had been to prevent tax evasion. In May 1728 Louis allowed the appeal, provided the bottled wine was moved in quantities of not less than 100 if for French consumption, or by 50 to 100 for export (a concession to the Treasury). The Champenois were, in fact, still endeavouring to reduce these amounts just before the Revolution of 1789, but by permitting movement of this, and only this, wine in bottles at all, the way had been opened for serious trading in sparkling champagne.

Louis passed a further piece of legislation in March 1735, which prescribed the size and content of a champagne bottle. Patrick Forbes writes: 'The King stipulated that it must in future weigh 25 ounces, contain exactly 1 Paris pint (about 1.6 imperial pints) and be tied down with three threaded string, well twisted and knotted in the form of a cross over the cork.' Sparkling champagne had come to stay.

This legislation concerned wine still being made as originally devised at the end of the seventeenth century. The wine was bottled before the finish of the only fermentation, using what today is called the *méthode rurale* or *ancestrale*, leaving the wine with a light sparkle but the wine was cloudy. The coming of the nineteenth century was to change the method drastically, but little by little. The first thirty to forty years of the new century witnessed the creation of a second fermentation and the production of a clear wine by driving the lees down into the neck of the bottle and expelling them.

From the beginning of the evolution of sparkling wine, sugar appears to have been added but simply to improve the wine's flavour. By 1718 it was being claimed that Dom Pérignon himself added sugar to the champagne, although this was strongly disputed later by Dom Grossard. Certainly the English wine merchants appear to have been aware of the use of sugar to create a stronger sparkle, since in a paper read to the newly formed Royal Society in 1662, Dr Merret referred to the large amounts of what he termed 'sugar molasses' added to wines to make them drink 'brisk and sparkling'.* Nevertheless the early addition of sugar to champagne wines appears to have been to round out their flavour and make them less tart.

In 1801 Jean-Antoine Chaptal published a treatise which covered cultivation of the vine and the art of winemaking. M. de Chaptal, a gifted chemist who also served Napoleon as Minister of the Interior, was apparently the first to understand the relationship between sugar and alcohol. The work of Louis Pasteur in clarifying the scientific basis of winemaking was still a good fifty years away. Chaptal, whose name is commemorated in the French term *chaptalisation*, urged upon winemakers (particularly those in cool northern regions) the advantages gained by adding sugar to the grape juice, or must, to raise the alcoholic degree of the finished wine.

From here it was a simple step for some winemakers in Champagne to experiment with the addition of sugar not only to the must, but also to still wine before bottling it, to see whether this would produce a good sparkle. The problem soon became apparent: how much sugar should be added? The system certainly

* See footnote to Chapter 4, p. 20.

worked, but too little sugar produced only faintly sparkling wines, while too much resulted in broken bottles and lost production.

In 1836 matters drastically improved. One of the unsung heroes of Champagne is Professor François of Châlons-sur-Marne (now Châlons-Champagne). A chemist by trade, Professor François worked out how to measure reasonably accurately the amount of sugar left in the wine at the finish of the original fermentation. His device, named the *sucre-œnomètre*, made it possible for a wine-maker to add a measured dose of sugar to produce a given pressure in the bottle. This reduced the scale of bottle breakage, but it had become apparent that the only long-term solution was for the glass makers to develop a bottle capable of withstanding higher pressure. By the mid-1850s, glass bottles strong enough to contain 6 atmospheres were being made. Ironically, M. François' system, the *réduction François*, was largely ignored in Champagne, and it was not until much later in the century that the deliberate use of the *liqueur de tirage* – a mixture of yeast, wine and sugar to stimulate the second fermentation – was widely used. In any case, the whole process of fermentation finally unveiled in 1859 by Pasteur was further developed by other scientists, notably a German named Büchner who, right at the end of the century, demonstrated for the first time that the main action on sugar in producing alcohol was not the yeast as such but substances called enzymes secreted by the yeasts. And finally, of enormous importance was the work of a Champenois called Manceau who, in 1900, devised an accurate method of calculating the amount of sugar needed to produce the correct mousse.

The second major advance in the method was the creation of a truly clear wine. The term for clearing a bottle of its dead lees is *dégorgement* (or disgorgement). A crude form had been practised from the very beginning. It appears that right from Pérignon's day there was a tendency to keep bottles of sparkling champagne neck-down in boxes of sand, or a similar substance. When required for drinking, these were brought to the table, still in an inverted position, where the cork was removed. The wine was either decanted into a clean container, thereby losing a great deal of its sparkle, or poured into glasses with hollow stems where much of the retained sediment would settle. Neither of these methods would produce a truly limpid wine, and the growing complaints about the cloudiness gradually led to an investigation into better methods, and finally to their commercial application.

The deep-seated problem lay in the fact that although the bulk of the sediment would, if the bottle was left inverted, sink into the neck, there were sticky elements which adhered to the side of the bottle and would not be moved. Just as the name of Dom Pérignon is forever attached, rightly or wrongly, to the creation of a sparkling wine, the name of the Veuve Clicquot is bracketed with *remuage* – the riddling method which finally enabled limpid sparkling wine to be produced.

In 1797 a young man named François, heir to the Clicquot businesses of banking, woollen manufacture and, as a secondary interest, champagne, met and fell in love with the daughter of a textile maker of Reims. Her name was Nicole-Barbe de Ponsardin. The following year the young couple married in a champagne cellar, as the churches were then closed following the Revolution. It appears to have been a very happy marriage, and the young couple were very involved with all aspects of the developing champagne trade. In 1806, when just thirty, François Clicquot died very suddenly of 'a malignant fever', and his heartbroken father prepared to close down the business. He reckoned without the determination of Nicole-Barbe, then only twenty-seven, who within four months had borrowed the money from her family and her in-laws, taken a business partner, arranged for the head of another champagne business to help in the blending of the wines, and restarted the company as Veuve Clicquot-Ponsardin, Fourneaux & Cie.

Just as the stories of Dom Pérignon have lost nothing in the telling, so neither, presumably, have those which attribute the discovery of *remuage* to the Veuve Clicquot. Mme Clicquot was certainly concerned about the cloudiness of the wine which, by the nineteenth century, was being criticised on the export markets, if not in Paris itself.

By 1806, within a year of her taking control of a major Champagne house, Reims was buzzing with rumours about the Veuve's kitchen table. According to the legend, at night Nicole-Barbe would go down to her kitchen table where she had carved holes to hold the bottles firmly upside-down. She would remove them on a regular basis, shake them to disturb the sediment, then replace them in the holes. This form of *remuage* was cumbersome and very slow. Moreover, a huge amount of space must have been involved; but it was the first step towards genuine *remuage*, which evolved somewhere between 1806 (when the rumours began) and 1818.

Evidence exists that the next step – modifying the process of shaking the bottle, to twisting and gradual tilting, which dispensed with the need to remove the bottle each time – was a development of the Widow's system by one of her employees, Antoine Müller, *chef des caves*. M. Müller seems to have realised that by carving the holes at a 45° angle, it was possible to move a bottle from a horizontal position to an almost vertical one, sending the sediment gradually down into the neck. Although this could be done if the boards were horizontal, pressure on space necessitated tilting them at an angle and thus was born the *pupitre*, comprising two boards hinged at the top to form a triangle. Müller left the Clicquot employ in 1822 to set up his own business, but he advertised the fact that he had been in charge of production at Veuve Clicquot for a while, creating a perfectly clear wine. On the heels of this the process became common knowledge. In modern parlance, no doubt it was 'leaked', but unlike use of the *liqueur de tirage*, which was almost ignored in Champagne until the 1880s (although widely used elsewhere as in Germany for sekt), *remuage* had been generally adopted by the 1850s.

Some form of *dégorgement* had been carried out from the very beginning, though often only by decanting from one bottle to another. The start of *dégorgement* as known today is first mentioned in 1813 by André Jullien, who also commented on the numerous gadgets developed for the topping-up of the bottles, a very tricky process which had to be carried out by hand with, at that time, sparkling wine.* *Dégorgement à la volée* – the removal of the sediment, topping-up and recorking 'by hand' – is still carried out occasionally, but as the champagne trade grew during the second half of the nineteenth century, the desirability of a faster method to cope with the sheer number of bottles required became obvious. In 1896 Armand Walfart patented the method still used today, known as *dégorgement à la glace*. In fact M. Walfart had invented it as early as 1884. It was first used in 1889 and was

---

* André Jullien, *Topography of All Known Vineyards*, London, 1824.

introduced into commercial use in 1891 by two champagne houses: Moët & Chandon and Perrier-Jouët.

Dégorgement à la glace evolved from a very simple idea. If the neck of the bottle could be dipped into a freezing solution of brine for long enough, the sediment on the cap and the small amount of wine surrounding it would form a slushy ice pellet, after which the bottle could be turned upright without the danger of the lees remixing with the wine. The *dégorgement*, whether by hand or machine, thus became a simple matter. This freezing system was soon shown to have one other major advantage. Although only the neck was subjected to the cooling process, it resulted in a lower temperature throughout the bottle, thus inhibiting the CO_2. This in turn meant that far less wine escaped, leading to less need for topping-up, and the loss of pressure was minimised.

As well as the major changes throughout the nineteenth century, there were other, if smaller, developments of great importance once the method itself had been so greatly improved.

A machine was developed which pre-washed the bottles before filling. Nicholas Faith, in his *Story of Champagne*, recounts how proud of their cleanliness the Champenois were, and how appalled one winemaker was to discover that in Paris the same water would be used to rinse many bottles. Another machine was developed to give the same measured dose of the final *liqueur d'expédition* to each bottle. Indeed, very similar small machines can still be seen today in many small houses in Champagne and in other French sparkling wine areas. Then the *dosage* (*liqueur d'expédition*) itself was vastly improved for the wines of the time. It must be stressed that today's is rather different. Then the *dosage* included, over and above the cane sugar and wine, some acid (tartaric or citric) if the acidity seemed low, a little tannin and some brandy to ensure the final alcoholic strength was as required.

Then there was the problem of the cork. To control the mousse within the bottle the cork had to be of good quality and to fit tightly. In the early days apparently the cork had been inserted and then pushed into place by the bottler using his teeth! Subsequently a hammer was designed for the job, but finally a suitable corking machine was developed in the 1820s. But then, as today, bad cork was a problem. It was found that if the corks were soaked in cold water for a time, not only were they easier to work with but the really bad ones turned dark and could be discarded. By the 1850s there were new glues which enabled corks to be made from more than one piece, and branding of the corks with the vintage or the name of the producer became possible.

In order to contain the pressure in a bottle, a champagne cork needs to be made from closely veined or 'hard' cork, difficult to obtain in large quantities. Thus the practice arose first of manufacturing the cork from two or three thinner strips glued together lengthways. Eventually there was insufficient hard cork even for this, so the modern or agglomerated cork was developed. The top part was made from compressed cork dust with two, or very occasionally three, discs of hard cork glued to the base and in contact with the wine.

The string ties laid down by Louis XV were now replaced with wire muzzles put on by machine, and the house of Jacquesson had designed and patented the idea of the capsules which cover the top of the cork. Today, these are highly collectable.

Finally the nineteenth century saw the evolution of dry champagne, another factor which had its origins in the British market. The removal by Mr Gladstone of the Imperial Preference in 1861 reduced the penal import duties levied against French wines. Additionally, his Single Bottle Act of the same year enabled the purchase of single bottles rather than entire cases, thus laying the foundation of the modern retail wine trade. The French, who had assumed that the palate across the Channel would have been ruined by the sweetness and alcoholic level of port, were proved wrong. Until about 1860 the great, and by now branded, champagnes had a fairly high sugar content. They were expected to be 'rich' in style, a term which almost certainly referred to the amount of sugar and brandy in the *dosage*. Today this style would be regarded as distinctly sweet, but it did have the advantage of enabling the wines to be drunk young, with no need for a long ageing period.

The idea of *brut* or dry champagne was effectively unknown. The first commercial reference appears in 1848 when a merchant called Burne, having sampled the 1846 Perrier-Jouët vintage without any added sugar, liked and shipped it, although it has to be added that his customers did not support his views. The first dry wine to have any real success appears to have been from the 1865 vintage, which also started the demand for special vintage years still with us today. Although it was relatively unsuccessful outside London, smart society in the capital was impressed, and finally the great 1874 wine from Pommery settled the matter. Dry champagne had arrived, and the sparkling wine first made in 1690 had evolved into the drink we recognise today.

It should not be assumed, however, that just because these critical developments took place during the last century the method used is written in tablets of stone. The twentieth century may not have seen such great leaps forward, but work has continued, some of which may drastically alter aspects of the modern method. Even a cursory glance at the steps of production pinpoints *remuage* as being the most laborious, and it is on this that most of the recent experimentation has taken place. It is important to understand that no alteration to the method would be permitted legally unless, after a long trial, it can be shown either to improve the final result or, at the very least, to make the process easier and keep the quality as high as it presently is.

The first development concerned automatic *remuage*, initially worked out in Spain for use in the huge Cava industry, where it is known as the *girasol*, or sunflower. This was adapted for Champagne by the firm of Georges Gardet. At its largest the *gyropalette* consists of a metal pallet which contains 504 bottles at a time. The shape is octagonal, and the bottles are placed neck downwards and moved normally every eight hours, either by a hand-controlled mechanism, or by a computer-controlled device affectionately known as a *pupimatic*. Remuage can thereby be completed in about one week, as opposed to the eight to ten weeks usually required by hand.

Given the time saving, it might be expected that the entire champagne industry would have turned to automation. This has not happened as opinions are divided between those makers who believe the *gyropalette* to give a better, cleaner and speedier result, and those convinced that traditional methods work best. The coming of mechanical *remuage* through *gyropalettes*, whether worked by hand or by computer, might have been thought to help solve the problem, but by no means all producers have been convinced about its efficacy. Some, like Piper-Heidsieck, now riddle all their wines in this manner; many more use it for NV wines, but not for vintage or special *cuvées*; yet others eschew it altogether and still employ a small army of *remueurs*. The size of the house concerned seems to have little bearing on the decision, but many do, in fact, hedge their bets, using the automatic method of *remuage* for the non-vintage wines, while retaining hand *remuage* in the traditional *pupitres* for the vintage and *cuvée de prestige* wines.

In 1975 came the new idea of encapsulating the yeast for the second fermentation inside an alginate bead. There are, however, experiments afoot that may make all current systems of *remuage* completely outdated. The first, and probably best known, is Les Billes. If the yeast could be imprisoned within a bead made from a polymer extracted from marine algae and constructed in such a way as to allow wine and carbon dioxide molecules to pass through it, while at the same time preventing the yeast sediment from settling outside the bead, then the problem of *remuage* would cease to exist. At the end of the maturation period the beads containing the yeast sediment, being heavier than the wine, would simply drop into the neck on the capsule as soon as the bottle was inverted.

It is a simple idea, but the technology took years to perfect, and even then years of trial vinification were necessary to ensure that the quality of the wine was not diminished. One of the major problems proved to be the design of a delicate machine capable of loading the correct number of beads into each bottle without breaking the alginate skin. At the start of the experimentation, the loading of the beads had to be done by hand. Today, however, a satisfactory prototype machine has been developed, and after nearly twenty years of trials, Moët & Chandon – who, along with the CIVC and INRA* carried out the research – are now between a pilot scheme and full production.

It may well be, as predicted by Tom Stevenson, that by the end of the century Les Billes will have made both the remaining *remueurs* and the *gyropalettes* redundant. But given the conservative nature of many of the Champenois, it is more likely that this will remain a third option, at least for the time being.

Another possible system, sometimes fondly named 'the Teabag', works on an almost similar idea. Here the yeasts for the second fermentation are placed in a cartridge, which is then slotted into the neck of the bottle. This system allows a similar contact between

* Comité Interprofessionnel du Vin de Champagne (see Chapter 12); Institut National de la Recherche Agronomique, the specialist organisation for research founded in 1946 and funded by the ministries for Scientific Research and Agriculture.

initially the yeast, then the lees, and the wine. The advantage here is that when ageing is complete, the cartridge can simply be withdrawn and the bottle topped up. No form of *remuage* is required whatsoever.

For a large number of years additives, such as bentonite, have been blended with the wine at bottling time, when the *cuvée* is made. The idea was to find out whether such additions could improve the ease of *remuage*. Out of this idea the Station Œnotechnique de Champagne, situated in Epernay, has produced a range of products branded under the commercial name of Adjuvant, which are blends of different amounts of bentonite and algae. These appear to have had a significant effect on the ease of and time taken in *remuage*, especially with the automatic method.

With modern scientific developments, the question inevitably arises: would not the simplest method of all be to use yeasts for the second fermentation which have been genetically engineered to let the lees simply fall on to the cap? Certainly this has been considered as a possibility and work done on this principle. The present situation is that development of such a yeast is a long-term project, as not only swift *remuage* but also, and most importantly, the aromas and flavours produced must be at least as good a standard as those of today.

Only the future will tell, but what is certain is that no alteration to the modern method, however clever or convenient, will be considered if there is the slightest danger to the quality of the finished drink.

7

The Modern Vineyard

The Revolution of 1789 was to change the face of the Champagne vineyard for ever, but did not affect the standing of the wines. In Patrick Forbes's evocation of this time he recounts how Mirabeau's brother was believed to drink two bottles of the wine with a meal. A cartoon shows his body as a cask and his legs as bottles, while one hand carries a glass and the other the bottle from which to fill it. Danton and Desmoulins shared a bottle of sparkling Aÿ before climbing aboard the tumbril for their journey to Madame la Guillotine.

This is to run ahead. The harvest of 1789 was disastrous. The weather had been appalling, with the previous winter the worst for about eighty years, followed by frosts which did not cease until 21 July. Nicholas Faith in his *Story of Champagne* quotes a letter from the Intendant for the region dated 21 October in which he wrote that the vintage, referred to as 'the principal product of Champagne', had to be effectively written off 'because it is barely a twelfth of the average and because adverse weather promises no possible quality, for the grapes, although still green and far from an acceptable degree of maturity, have all been affected by rot'. This disaster, accompanied by a social collapse leading, among other things, to failure in food distribution, resulted in near famine and widespread misery.

Until this time, apart from the great estates owned by families such as the Brularts, Marquises of Sillery, by and large the Champagne vineyards were worked by the peasantry and the wines made by the monks. The monasteries owned many vineyards, (often willed to them in return for perpetual prayers or masses), but under the *ancien régime* the small vignerons were legally prevented from acquiring further vineyards. This law was repealed by the Revolutionary government so that the land confiscated at the closure of the monasteries or from the original aristocratic owners could now be purchased, but the misery of the time and lack of any capital on the part of the people now entitled to buy, prevented most from doing so. Any money available was needed to buy food.

Most of the confiscated lands, therefore, were parcelled out to those interested, the great estates and monastic holdings were destroyed, and the immediate and long-term effect of this was to tip the balance of power in the winemaking world very strongly in favour of the merchants, especially those already established, among them Ruinart, the oldest of the houses. This situation was strongly reinforced during the Napoleonic era.

Only one new firm was founded during the Revolutionary years, Boizel. By the turn of the century, Claude Jacquesson had opened his business, while Jean-Rémy Moët and Veuve Cliquot flourished both at home and on the export market during Napoleonic times, with the Prince Regent in 1806 ordering 2,000 bottles from Moët. Two other major houses were also started: Henriot and Perrier Jouët. The era of the big producing house and its branded name had arrived and the pattern of the Champagne trade had been established.

The modern pattern of the vineyards, however, was still some way off. In 1834 a fungal disease was discovered and investigated in the United States. In 1845 an English gardener by name of Tucker found some diseased leaves at Margate. These were identified by a curate who was fascinated by all forms of fungi, but most particularly by those which cause disease in plants. He named it *Oidium tuckeri* after Mr Tucker. Later it was found not to be an original species, but belonged to the genus *Uncinula* and given the specific name of *necator*. It is usually known as powdery mildew and is a major disease in humid climates. Nowadays it can be treated easily and as a matter of course by spraying or dusting with sulphur, but its arrival from the USA caused serious problems in the European vineyards. By 1852 it was endemic throughout Europe and North Africa. A dust-like white coating appears on the leaves and the developing grapes, which may well split but do not ripen. It does not, however, attack fruit which is past *véraison* (the time of ripening when the grapes turn colour), nor does it kill the vine – as the next plague was to do. Nevertheless, it did create huge problems and panic in the vineyards, until sulphur dust came into general and successful use by 1863.

In *The Great Wine Blight* George Ordish calls it a rehearsal for what was to come, mainly because the idea of using science to combat such diseases was new and had been shown to work, and many who had helped in this instance were also to be involved with the next disaster which was to strike when the vineyards had barely recovered. By the late 1860s, authenticated reports of an unknown disease were appearing. Although by no means the first rumour, a letter was written by a veterinarian called Delorme to the President of the Agricultural Show Society of Aix and dated 8 November 1867, which described in detail the devastation of a recently planted vineyard in the area. The accuracy of his description was amazing. The vines had produced well in 1865. By August 1866 a large number showed advanced symptoms and by February 1867 those affected were dead – the speed probably owing to the extreme youth of the vines. Initial theories that it was some form of tree root rot, caused by honey fungus, were soon disproved, and the disease appeared to spread at an alarming rate.

A commission was set up in 1868, a member of which was M. Planchon, Professor of Pharmacy at Montpellier University. The commission did not waste time. Having established that the roots of dead vines gave no indication of the problem, they dug out apparently healthy ones too and eventually found that the roots of living but affected plants were covered with small yellow insects. M. Planchon realised that it was necessary to follow the life cycle of this insect, suspecting that a winged form must exist. Duly, one obliged. In his own words, it hatched into 'an elegant little aphid with four feet and transparent wings'. To combat this devastating pest, it now became essential to trace its full life cycle and discover any weak link. The battle against what Planchon named *Phylloxera vastatrix* was on.

Incredible as it may seem, little interest was initially taken by the press, the public, or even the government, until it became obvious that this new pest was spreading. By 1872 it had reached Bordeaux, and by mid-1873 the government was prepared to offer a very large reward for a cure – no less than 300,000 francs. Numerous treatments were offered. In less than two years, 696 suggestions were sent for testing, including burying live toads to extract the poison! One or two did appear to be more efficacious.

Flooding, for example, kept the pest at bay, but vines do not like wet feet. Carbon disulphide worked, but, as a nerve poison, is highly dangerous. Meanwhile, it had been noticed that American vines remained healthy – the idea of grafting *vinifera* vines on to American rootstock followed. Slow and difficult though early grafting was, Europe's vineyards now had a future.

Initially, as phylloxera moved into the warm southern areas, the belief among the Champenois was that they were too far north and too cold to be in peril. Then, in August 1890, it was identified in the Marne at Vincelles. Gaston Chandon de Briailles purchased the property and destroyed the vines in the vain hope that this might save the region from the pest. Initially, there was swift action. A group to control the attack was set up, with the intention of destroying affected vines and paying compensation, but in practice little was achieved. Beset by quarrels and bureaucratic delays, the concerted action needed never materialised, partly because small vignerons distrusted the motives of the large commercial houses and believed that their true objective was to destroy them.

So the pest was allowed free rein, and eventually, as in other areas, it became obvious that all vines would have to be replanted on to American rootstocks. Curiously there are two small vineyard areas, both owned by the house of Bollinger, which have remained phylloxera-free. Both grow Pinot Noir. One is at Aÿ and the other near Bouzy. Visitors interested to see how the Champagne vineyards once looked should visit them. Compared with the neat, serried ranks of vines elsewhere, these tiny areas look overgrown and very untidy, for the vines grow in the old manner on their roots. When a new plant is needed, a suitable branch is pushed into the earth, where it develops new roots and can be cut off to form a new plant. Moreover, vines grown this way live far longer than the 25 to 35 years allotted to most champagne vines. However, this system precludes mechanisation of any kind, so even if by some miracle phylloxera were to die out, such a method could never be revived.

One immediate effect of the phylloxera crisis, and not only in Champagne, was a great shortage of wine, and this increased the hostility between the small growers and the merchants, some of whom were observed to be selling many more bottles than had in fact been produced. In a way this was understandable. Demand for champagne was rising sharply at a time when the vineyards were being replanted, which meant a five-year break in the production of grapes. So other sources were sought and while some merchants were buying from vineyards in the Aisne round Château-Thierry, not then considered as part of viticultural Champagne, others were undoubtedly looking farther afield for their base wines. One well-respected firm openly purchased in Chablis and yet others were believed to source as far away as the Midi.

All of this was driving the small growers to despair. Replanting was slow, poverty was marked, yet some merchants were buying grapes from 'foreign' vineyards and then paying only low prices for the grapes from the Marne area itself. It was a recipe for disaster.

By the early part of this century, almost everyone concurred that an agreement which legally defined the champagne-grape area was essential. However, in 1905 the government, which was becoming increasingly concerned about the amount of fraudulent wines from all great areas on sale, missed a tremendous opportunity. On 1 August 1905, a law establishing a central body responsible for the repression of fraud was promulgated. The all-important question of delimited boundaries of the various regions was dodged. Such questions were now the responsibility of the local administration.

The champagne merchants already had their Syndicat du Commerce, founded in 1884, and their Association Viticole Champenoise, disliked by the growers in spite of the AVC's efforts to help them replant. Eventually, in 1904, the growers formed their own federation, the Syndicat Général des Vignerons, whose declared aim was to ensure that the grower received a fair price for his grapes. Neither side appreciated the 1905 law.

The next few years were complicated by dissension among the growers. On the one side were those from the Aube, who were determined that their vineyards should be included in any legal definition of the area, pointing out that historically the region had always been part of Champagne. Ranged against them were the growers from the Marne, who showed that, traditionally, Champagne's reputation rested on wines from that department only; the inclusion of Aube wine in the *cuvée* was of recent origin and a result of the crisis in the vineyards. The hostility between the parties led to government intervention. The bill of 17 December 1908 published the approved vineyard area. The Marne and the Aisne were included; the Aube, not mentioned. Naturally the Aubois were furious, although in fact their wine was still flowing into a number of cellars in Reims and Epernay.

There followed another blow – three consecutive vintages culminating in 1910 saw some vineyards unable to harvest a single bunch of grapes. By 1911 many were facing bankruptcy and the whole district had become a powder keg waiting for the tinder box.

From 4 November 1910, unrest was prevalent in the Marne villages, aggravated by a refusal to pay taxes and threats against merchants believed to be acting fraudulently. Then, on 17 January 1911, a crowd of vignerons destroyed thousands of bottles of wine. Troops were moved into the area and Epernay was sealed off, since the 'foreign' wine arrived at its railway station. The Prefect of the Marne promised the growers he would prevent any further wine arriving if the violence stopped, and indeed he did try to do this.

Finally, on 11 February, the government provided the flash point. A law further restricting the use of imported wine in champagne *cuvées* reached the statute book. Troops were withdrawn, but the Aube had yet again been totally excluded. Without instant communication, it took a little while for this to penetrate to the growers of the Aube, but when it did rebellion was in the air. On 27 March the Red Flag flew in Bar-sur-Aube and the Internationale was sung. In Troyes, the ancient capital of the region, demonstrations were held and civil disorder was rife: tax forms were burnt as was an effigy of the Prime Minister.

Panicked by such a show of anger, the government backed down and tried to repeal the laws of 1908 and 1911, but this made matters worse. On receipt of this news, on 10 April, the rage of the vignerons of the Marne finally erupted. The results were the Aÿ riots, the sheer viciousness of which stunned the rest of France. The tocsin sounded and armed vine-growers first attacked premises in Dizy and then Damery. By midday on the 12th, the mob had entered Aÿ which was systematically looted, innocent merchants and suspected fraudsters alike – although the firm of Bollinger was spared, the mob dipping their flag as they passed. Vines and wine were destroyed, houses and warehouses set alight, before the rioters moved towards their main destination: Epernay. Here, at last, they were checked by soldiers. The riot transformed the region into an armed camp. According to reports, troops were brought in and billeted in every village while order was restored. Indeed, the army

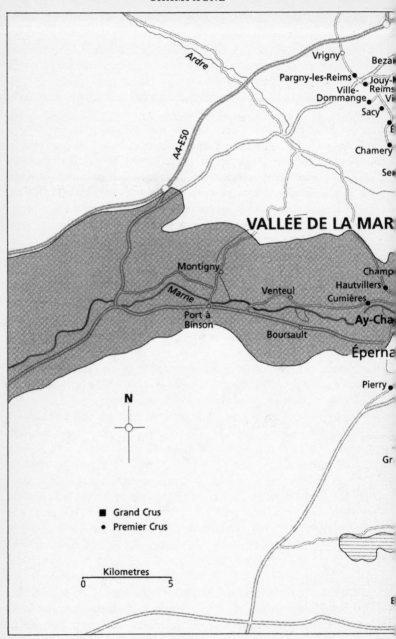

Vrigny

Beza

Pargny-les-Reims

Jouy-
Reims

Ville-
Dommange

Vi

Sacy

E

Chamery

Se

VALLÉE DE LA MAR

Montigny

Champ

Venteul

Hautvillers

Cumières

Marne

Port à
Binson

Boursault

Ay-Cha

Éperna

Pierry

N

Gr

■ Grand Crus
● Premier Crus

Kilometres
0   5

E

REIMS

Cormontreuil
Taissy
Trois-Puits
Sillery
Puisieulx
ontbré
Beaumont-sur-Vesle
ers-
rand
Rilly-la-
Montagne
Chigny-
les-Roses
Ludes
Verzenay
Mailly-
Champagne
Verzy
Villers-
Marmery
Vesle
MONTAGNE DE REIMS

Trepail
Billy-le-Grand
Vaudemanges
Louvois
Tauxieres-Mutry
Bouzy
Abonnay
Avenay
Mutigny
Tours-sur-Marne
Mareuil-sur-Ay
Bisseuil
A4-E50

Oiry
houilly
A26

Marne

CÔTE DES BLANCS

amant
Avize
Oger
le Mesnil-sur-Oger
Châlons-sur-Marne

Villeneuve-
Renneville
ertus
Voipreux

Bergeres-les-Vertus
Coligny

only left when their accommodation was required to house the other army: the grape pickers. A number of arrests were made and prison sentences followed. The ringleaders were tried some months later at a distance; one was acquitted and a few imprisoned. Three people died, one from wounds and the other two, among the accused, committed suicide by hanging. There was considerable damage to property, vines and training posts, and a great deal of wine was destroyed. But the violence could have resulted in far greater loss of life, and even today the suspicion lingers that much of the trouble may have been caused by political agitators from Paris taking advantage of the widespread sense of despair.

After the riots, the government rethought its policies and on 7 June, just two months after the events, produced a new bill. This recognised two levels of champagne: first were those named in the decree of 1908; second, an area to be known as Champagne Deuxième Zone which covered most of the Aube, and those other communes in the Marne and the Aisne not included in 1908. This compromise, probably inoperable in practice, seemed to satisfy both parties, but it was still being discussed and had not yet become law when the First World War broke out in 1914.

In 1919 the matter again came up for consideration and the new government amended the bill of 1911. Now, for the first time, the idea of an *appellation* as we would recognise it today took form, but lacked substance until 1935. Nonetheless, the idea of a two-tier Champagne was rather cunningly dropped as such and the whole matter of the Aube versus the Marne was neatly removed from governmental authority and handed to the law courts. Legal battles raged for six years, but finally the courts decided that the Aubois were in the right, and so in 1927 there was a new decree setting out the communes which would be entitled to produce grapes for champagne.

All the vineyards in the region have an official classification. Known as the *échelle des crus*, the lowest-rated today are at 80 per cent, while just seventeen of the villages stand on the peak at 100 per cent. This is not a new idea. Certain *crus* have been outstanding from the beginning. During the eighteenth century these included Aÿ and Sillery, long considered the finest, to which were added Cramant, Avise, Le Mesnil, Oger and Hautvillers, among others. By 1875, for example, a local trade publication named Aÿ and Verzenay, plus Cramant, as top *crus*.

The *échelle des crus* has its origins in 1919. For the first time, serious negotiations between growers and merchants created a ranking which, with a few exceptions, remains true today. The influential magazine, *La Revue de Champagne*, sees the *échelle* not so much as a ladder but as a pyramid. There are 319 villages in the entire region, giving 336 separate *crus*. The disparity in the numbers results from the fact that a few villages have two separate levels of *cru*, depending on the grapes grown. For example, in Tours-sur-Marne the Pinot Noir vineyards are rated 100 per cent while Chardonnay achieves only 90 per cent, or Chouilly where the Chardonnay rates 100 per cent, but Pinot Noir only 95 – so in each case creating two separate *crus* for one village.

Resting on the peak on the pyramid are the 17 *grands crus* rated at 100 per cent. Interestingly enough, 13 of these were rated as *grands crus* in 1919. Listed alphabetically, today they are Ambonnay, Avize, Aÿ, Beaumont-sur-Vesle, Bouzy, Chouilly, Cramant, Louvois, Mailly-Champagne, Le Mesnil-sur-Oger, Oger, Oiry, Puisieulx, Sillery, Tours-sur-Marne, Verzenay, Verzy. The size of this group is the result of an upgrading of 5 hitherto *premiers crus* villages in 1985. Suddenly, without any previous announcement, Chouilly, Le Mesnil-sur-Oger, Oger, Oiry and Verzy joined the original 12 *grands crus* which had remained unchanged for forty years. No explanation was given at the time, and none has been forthcoming, although for many years the high quality of the grapes here had been obvious.

The next level covers the communes rated as *premiers crus*,* at between 90 and 99 per cent on the scale. Here 39 named villages have between them 43 *premiers crus*, again related to the grapes grown as previously shown. It is interesting, particularly in view of the earlier history of the region, that all the *crus* in both the Aube and the other three departments (Aisne, Haute-Marne and Seine-et-Marne) are simply AOC Champagne, rated at between 80 and 89 per cent, and that to find an 80 per cent rating it is necessary to look at the Aube. The simple AOC level also covers those communes not listed in the *grands* or *premiers crus* in the Marne itself.

Of the total 31,050 hectares that could be in production at any given time, only 4,500 are *grands crus*, the most sought-after

---

* For a complete list, see Appendix 6.

grapes, particularly by the major houses. The *premiers crus*, including the two rated at 99 per cent – Mareuil-sur-Aÿ and Tauxières – have between them 5,700 hectares. The importance of the *échelle* is that it once dictated the price that would have been paid by the houses for the grapes. The higher the rating, the more expensive the grapes. However, since the introduction of a free market in grapes following the collapse of the old Contract system (see Chapter 12), the *échelle* has no longer completely regulated the price.

The question therefore arises: is the *échelle des crus* a fair system? There is probably no comprehensive answer to this. By giving the rating to a commune, it then covers all vineyards within it and undoubtedly there will be variations in quality. It is difficult to see how this could be avoided, except by complicating what is essentially a straightforward and reasonably sensible system. Imagine the chaos that would reign if each commune were reassessed and different ratings placed on individual tiny plots. Nonetheless, there is possibly a case for arguing that a handful, certainly among the top-rated villages, could produce some named *lieux-dits*, since some growers in, say, *premier cru* vineyards do produce grapes at least as good certain *grands crus*.

An interesting example of this relates to the little-known area of Montgueux in the Côte des Bars. The village produces high-quality Chardonnay on particularly favourable slopes, but is rated only at 80 per cent. The Chardonnay produced here is highly sought after, enabling the owners to obtain higher prices than the *échelle* warrants. Why, then, has it not been upgraded? This is merely one instance among many, but it does focus on the question of whether the *échelle des crus* is overdue for a revamp. This would be extremely complicated – after all, no one has managed to produce a better system to replace the 1855 Bordeaux classification, based on commercial prices paid over a ten-year period. Undoubtedly, however, there are anomalies, which almost certainly arise from the strong feelings of nearly a century ago, that it was the department of the Marne that produced the best champagne. Technical advances in viticulture may mean this is no longer the case, but the old prejudices run deep.

8

Vine Varieties

As we have seen, one of the undoubted legacies of Dom Pérignon is the knowledge that a blending of the wines from different vine-yards was nearly always superior to the wine from a single vineyard. This was passed down as received wisdom, most notably in a letter written by the last cellarer of the Abbey of Hautvillers in 1821. Dom Grossard wrote: 'By blending in this way plainly different grape varieties as well as vineyards were involved.'

There is no means of knowing for certain which grape varieties were grown at the time of Dom Pérignon, for no one can truly identify the white varieties referred to as fromantius, moriband and jeunesse in Brother Pierre's *Treatise on Viticulture*. Yet we can surmise that, as one of Dom Pérignon's many achievements appears to have been the first making of truly red wines as well as clear white ones (as opposed to *vin gris* from red grapes), the district then, as today, grew both red and white varieties. Since 1927, when the law was first promulgated, there have been three classic grape varieties allowed for the making of champagne: red Pinot Noir, a related variety recognised for three or four centuries, Pinot Meunier, and finally white Chardonnay. Bearing in mind that cham-pagne is normally a blended wine, each of these grape varieties brings some special character to the finished product. Pinot Noir is a noble variety of great distinction, the source of all red burgundy apart from Beaujolais, and at its best capable of producing rich, long-lived velvety wines. Most of champagne's fame appears to have been based on this variety which gives both strength and backbone to the blends – the body and grip, as it were, in the mouth. The changing taste of champagne today means that lighter styles than those produced earlier this century are more in demand, so perhaps the Pinot Noir has lost some of its predominance, but it does remain an essential part of any fine, blended style.

It is a difficult grape to grow in such a northerly region, being sufficiently delicate to cause problems in severe winters such as 1984–85 when it was estimated that at least one in ten of Champagne's vines was killed by the cold. In addition, it buds early thus making spring frosts a very real hazard. It is highly susceptible to botrytis, always a danger in the cool, often damp conditions found so far north. On the other hand, it is also an early-ripening variety and does seem to give its very best in cooler areas. The long slow ripening brings elegant, almost luscious, fruit when conditions are favourable, as on the Côte d'Or or, further afield, in Oregon and Tasmania.

At present, about 36 per cent of the Champagne vineyard is planted with Pinot Noir, but of this percentage it is currently estimated that 40 per cent comes from the southern Aube district, where the soil and climatic differences certainly seem to suit the variety. It is well worth noting that the Aube was once very much Gamay country and that it was only from the 1950s onwards that Pinot Noir came to dominate.

In contrast to the undoubted star quality of Pinot Noir, its cousin, Pinot Meunier, is largely regarded as an inferior and much more rustic grape. Indeed, the pricing policy for these two grapes still supports that view, but during the last ten to fifteen years there has been a major reappraisal of Pinot Meunier, not before time considering that it represents 38 per cent of the plantings. Its home territory is the Valley of the Marne, a frost pocket and therefore highly unsuitable for Pinot Noir. The Meunier has the advantage of later budding and a more general resistance to cold. It takes the name 'meunier' or 'miller' from the underside of the leaves – they look as if they have been dusted with flour.

As a grape it is far less fussy than Pinot Noir and adapts itself readily to different sites. No wonder it is a favourite with the growers as it ripens well even in poor years, has good acidity and is generally amenable. Possibly its traditional bad name among winemakers arose from the fact that of the three grapes it needs the most careful handling. Moët & Chandon's Richard Geoffroy, who has long considered running a Meunier conference, is clear that, well handled, it gives an excellent wine, but otherwise it gives a coarse one and this is certainly borne out by many of the cheap champagnes which rely heavily upon the grape.

Among its admirers, the House of Krug use a good percentage of it, usually about 15 per cent, in their Grande Cuvée, although their source for Pinot Meunier is Leuvrigny, situated on the south bank of the Marne and an otherwise fairly unremarkable area. Other major quality houses also source their Pinot Meunier there, indicating that the quality of the wine produced depends not only on the handling, but also on the mesoclimate of the vineyard concerned.

The main complaint levelled at Pinot Meunier is that it does not age well, but handled well it gives a fresh fruitiness and the glorious aroma of rising dough or a freshly baked loaf, as Serena Sutcliffe sees it, and whereas until about ten years ago many houses denied using anything but Pinot Noir and Chardonnay in their wines, today most are happy to admit its usage in their blends – NV, at least. But the shadow of 'for early drinking only' undoubtedly still remains in spite of the fact that Krug is one of the longest-lived champagnes in existence.

The third grape is Chardonnay, currently the most popular white *cépage* in the world, the raw material of some of the greatest white wines made, including the Montrachets and Cortons Charlemagne of Burgundy. In the Champagne vineyard it accounts for around 26 per cent, certainly under 30 per cent of the plantings. Originally named apparently *Epinette*, it has been around in the region for two or three hundred years, but has only come into high popularity since the Second World War. Before that, the popular champagne taste was for the more overtly fruity Pinot styles. However, the popularity of the *blanc de blancs* wines and the blended lighter styles with high Chardonnay content has changed the view of Chardonnay in Champagne. Indeed, as Nicholas Faith points out, with the number of *blanc de blancs* champagnes currently being made, there have to be grave doubts about the Chardonnay percentages claimed for some of the blended NV styles.

Chardonnay too, like Pinot Meunier, tends to be a vine-grower's delight. Provided its roots are not too damp and the soil is not heavy clay, it is an adaptable variety and, very importantly, resistant to cold winter temperatures. It is early-budding and therefore susceptible to spring frosts, but it also ripens early making it suitable for the cooler northern areas, although it is sensitive to grey rot and powdery mildew in a humid climate. Unfortunately, it is also particularly prone to a viral disorder called fan leaf, or *court-noué*, which has caused great problems here and in Burgundy. Infection is spread by nematodes, microscopic organisms present in the soil. Once infected, the vines appear stunted with deformed fan-like leaves, yields are reduced and the plants eventually succumb. At present, clonal selection of virus-resistant stock, together with the use of a nematode-resistant rootstock, such as SO4, offers the best protection.

Chardonnay brings elegance, finesse and a degree of steeliness to the blends, as well as giving light, dry and crisp wines on its own. In spite of the lightness, some *blanc de blancs* are capable of developing over years into rich, harmonious wines of great depth, although most are made for relatively early drinking.

Its natural home is on the chalk slopes south of Epernay, the well-named Côtes des Blancs around Avize and the slopes around Cramant. Nonetheless, some very fine Chardonnay is grown on the Montagne de Reims – and the Dom Ruinart is an excellent example of how very fine these can be, while the Côtes de Sézanne also produce excellent Chardonnay. In spite of claims to the contrary, the Aube is really not particularly suited to this variety although one or two pockets of good Chardonnay are grown.

There remain, however, small pockets of other grape varieties once grown although these may not be replanted. They are Arbanne, Petit Meslier and Pinot Blanc Vrai. In 1927 the law stipulated four grape varieties: Pinot, presumably covering both Noir and Meunier, Chardonnay, Petit Meslier and Arbanne. Little of the last two remain. Some Petit Meslier grows in the Aube and a tiny amount in the Marne Valley, but it remains a difficult grape to graft, giving small yields and very high acidity. Arbanne appears to have been highly regarded last century. It is very aromatic and could easily overwhelm a blend. Only a very tiny number of plants remain and these inevitably will disappear when their life cycle is finished.

Some Pinot Blanc Vrai can still be found, but only negligible amounts. As for many years Chardonnay was frequently named Pinot Chardonnay before it was shown to be a different variety, many growers must have planted Pinot Blanc believing it to be one and the same. But with the work carried out on clones, and stock for replanting being bench-grafted, it seem likely that this *cépage* will also vanish from the Champagne vineyards.

Finally there remains a little Gamay. This variety had been widely grown in the Aube, but was omitted from the approved list of varieties in 1927. Initially, all vines were to disappear within eighteen years, but in practice a few still exist. The final date for uprooting was extended to 1952, but even then, possibly to protect the elderly, Gamay vines were permitted in the Aube only if they had been planted before 1948 and the owner was at least sixty in 1952. Thus the last few Gamay vines will shortly disappear, although in practice most of the Aube vineyards were replanted with Pinot Noir during the 1950s as it was recognised that, for champagne, Gamay was a most inferior grape.

Work on the various clones of the three classic grape varieties came late to Champagne. It was not really until the 1960s, although it is clear that the growers were aware of the differences between at least some of the Pinots. André Simon, writing in that decade, names the Plant Doré, commenting that there were three slightly different types of this variety, each of which had a different name: the Petit Plant Doré, the Gros Plant Doré d'Aÿ and le Vrai Doré, sometimes called Plant d'Aÿ. Then there was the Plant Gris, not to be confused with Pinot Gris, and the Plant de Vertus. He further makes it clear that these were all Pinot Noir clones and that Meunier as such was seen as a separate variety. Much early work appears to have been geared towards establishing whether there was a Pinot clone suitable for the frost pocket of the Marne Valley, thus enabling the noble variety to be planted when the Pinot Meunier vines needed to be uprooted. In practice however, as the work developed, so emphasis has switched to finding the best possible clones of each of the three varieties – Pinots Noir and Meunier and Chardonnay – and matching them to the conditions of both soil and climate in each of the individual vineyard areas. This work is still continuing.

Since the arrival of phylloxera in Champagne in 1870, as with all other areas, it has been necessary for all plants to be grafted on to American rootstock. Early in the fight against this louse it was discovered that there were three vines particularly resistant: *vitis berlandieri*, *vitis riparia* and *vitis rupestris*. One early discovery, however, was that these American rootstocks were less resistant to a high lime content in the soil than the original *vitis vinifera* varieties. Today, hundreds of rootstocks have been developed for different purposes, but those most effective against phylloxera have at least one of these three in their parentage.

In addition to protection against phylloxera, a rootstock selected for Champagne must be compatible with climate and soil as well as with the vine variety. As has been seen, the Champagne soils contain a very high proportion of chalk. Such a soil can result in chlorosis of the vine, leading to a yellowing of the foliage due to lack of chlorophyll, which in turn, on soils high in limestone, is usually caused by iron deficiency.

It is therefore essential that the rootstocks for Champagne have a resistance to phylloxera and lime. Of the varieties permitted the most widely used are 41B Millardet which is highly resistant to lime, SO4 (Selection Oppenheim de Teleki no. 4) and 3309 Couderc, the latter two giving medium resistance.

Grafting simply means putting together two pieces of plant material so that they weld together and form one; this has been an integral part of viticulture since the second half of the last century when it was shown to be the only effective weapon against the depredations of phylloxera. There are many different techniques to achieve this. Originally grafting occurred in the vineyard by planting the rootstock out in the autumn and grafting the scion variety on to it the following spring – a system known as 'field grafting'. Today, by far the most common method used is indoor 'bench grafting', frequently carried out by machines which join together the rootstock and scion usually with an omega-shaped cut. Thus, the vineyard owner will place an order with his supplier stating which clone is required on which rootstock.

Before the advent of phylloxera, the vine frequently lived for fifty to 100 years and possibly longer. Since the introduction of grafting, the life of most vines has been significantly shortened as the act itself impairs the flow of sap. Today, in commercial terms, the vine's life is reckoned to be about thirty-five years with the most productive period being between ten and twenty-five years of age, at which time it is making its strongest growth and producing the maximum weight of fruit.

Such prolific growth necessitates control, as otherwise all the strength of the plant would create green growth at the expense of ripening the fruit. Wild vines in the Middle East, for example, are not pruned but frequently scramble up the nearest host tree producing a plethora of tiny bunches at the end of the branches which reach the sun. The main reason for pruning, therefore, is simple. If left to its own devices the vine would throw out suckers from its base, it would develop huge new branches, and any fruit that got the chance to set would be small and probably never ripen. It is fair to say here that recent experiments have been carried out to see whether, left to itself, the vine could produce a natural balance of green growth and fruit, but so far the answer appears to be in the negative.

This has been understood almost from time immemorial. There is a delightful old myth which says that Bacchus was a chubby human baby who saw a bunch of beautiful ripe grapes hanging from the end of a vine branch which had scrambled all through a host tree, unchecked by any form of training. The baby Bacchus somehow scrambled up the tree and along the branch. Just as he stretched out to grasp the bunch, the branch broke under his weight and the baby fell from on high. But very luckily a passing god disliked the inevitable outcome, caught the baby and transformed him into a god. Thereafter Bacchus made certain his followers understood the importance of strong pruning of the vine, near the earth, so that such an accident should never happen again. The much later legend of St Martin of Tours and his donkey also preaches the same doctrine, namely that hard pruning produces fine grapes, and experience shows that fine grapes are needed to produce great wines. It appears that one day St Martin was visiting a neighbouring abbey and inspecting the vineyards and cellars. His donkey, left tethered near to some vines and bored with waiting for his master, sated his hunger on the nearest available vines. Legend does not record the fate of the beast, but the chewed plants produced the choicest grapes of all.

A further objective of pruning is to enable the vine to be trained into particular shapes which, in the AOC areas of France, such as Champagne, are deemed to have stood the test of time and quality, and are incorporated into the wine regulations for the district. All pruning and training systems fall under one of two main types: they are either spur or cane pruned. To understand the difference between the two methods, it is important to realise that the grapes will only be formed from shoots of that year, which grow from buds which develop on one-year-old wood. Sometimes this wood is a short spur with two (and very occasionally three) buds. In this case, whatever the name given to the training system, the vine has been spur pruned. At other times the one-year-old wood is in the form of a long cane with a larger number of buds, normally between five and fifteen, the cane being renewed each year. In this instance the vine is cane pruned.

In Champagne there are four permitted systems, although two do predominate. They are Cordon du Royat, Guyot (named after the French viticulturist who, in 1860, did much to formalise cane pruning), Taille Chablis and Vallée de la Marne. Apart from Guyot, all are spur-pruning systems.

The choice of system is related to both the grape variety and the vineyard's position on the *échelle des crus*. Thus, in all vineyards rated between 90 and 100 per cent the choice is between the Taille Chablis and the Cordon du Royat for all three grape varieties. In lesser-rated slopes, between 80 and 89 per cent, the Guyot is permitted, while for the Pinot Meunier only, at these lesser *échelles*, there is the possibility of using the Vallée de la Marne system.

In practice, however, it is usual for Cordon du Royat to be used for Pinot Noir on the Montagne de Reims and the Taille Chablis for the Chardonnay, particularly on the Côtes des Blancs – although nearly all Chardonnay is on this system – while Pinot Meunier in the lesser-rated areas of the Marne Valley will often use the Vallée de la Marne.

The Cordon du Royat system is based on a single branch trained horizontally on wires no more than 0.6 metres above the soil. This branch is allowed shoots on the upper side which must be at least 15cm apart, and each shoot carries a maximum of two buds. In the case of Chardonnay pruned this way, three buds are permitted, since the first one on this variety is always infertile. At the end of this branch there is a final shoot which looks like an extension of the main branch and this is permitted to carry four or five buds, depending on the variety.

Taille Chablis, as its name suggests, was developed last century in Chablis. It is generally recognised as the best method for Chardonnay, although slightly more difficult to manage since it can have up to five main branches. Each branch can have, in the case of Chardonnay, five buds (four for other varieties). As this is a spur-pruning system, the branches are grown at yearly intervals.

The Guyot method may be simple or double: one or two annually replaced canes, respectively, with a maximum permitted number

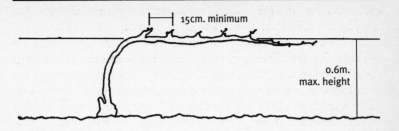

Cordon du Royat

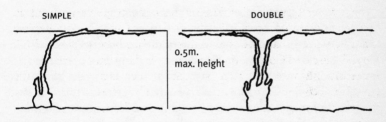

Guyot

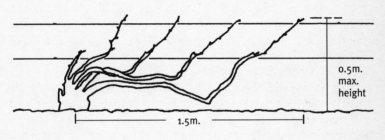

Taille Chablis

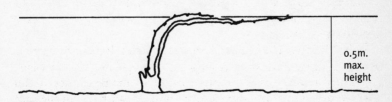

Vallée de la Marne

Pruning and training systems

59

of shoots. Guyot single allows ten buds; the double system, two canes with eight buds on each.

The Vallée de la Marne is allowed for Pinot Meunier only, in vineyards rated at 89 per cent or less. It is a complex system with a number of possible variations, but the basic and most usually found version allows a permanent branch with up to six shoots, while a secondary one can have ten buds.

On a journey through these vineyards, the first-time visitor always comments on the closeness of the vines. The spacing, between both vines and rows, is strictly controlled. Between the rows it is a maximum of 1.5 metres while, as already stated, between individual vines it can vary between just under 1 metre and 1.5 metres. This, of course limits the amount of mechanical work that can be done in the vineyard. However, experiments undertaken by the CIVC in past years have indicated that, for example, mechanical picking has an adverse effect. Thus, for the foreseeable future, apart from ploughing and spraying which these spaces allow, the present density will remain.

9

A Year in the Vineyards

The vineyards are at their most spectacular in the weeks after harvest as the leaves have turned to a magnificent mixture of red, russet orange and yellow, waiting for the first sharp frost before they fall. And this can be very sudden. On the morning after a frost the leaves can still glow under a clear sky, but by late afternoon the vines may be almost bare.

November is the start of the viticultural year, as the cold weather closes in and the sap dies down. During the month, the vineyards are dotted with growers cutting back the long whippy shoots, partly to prevent any high winds catching them and causing damage, and partly to clear the way for the all-important fertilisation to take place along uncluttered rows. Frequently the workers are accompanied by smoke as the cut prunings are burnt, for two reasons: plant hygiene (any lurking disease does not get the chance to over-winter) and to create potash to add to the soil as fertiliser.

Contrary to an often expressed view which arises from the idea that the best soil for good grapes is always poor, it is sometimes believed that vines are not fertilised. In Champagne the soil is very poor but intensely planted and supports a relatively high yield; fertilisation is a priority so that, while growth is dormant, the roots can search out new sources of food to help produce the next year's grapes.

All plants require certain chemical elements to survive. Nitrogen encourages green growth, potassium helps to enrich the sap, thus indirectly affecting the quality of the next vintage, and phosphorus assists root development, encouraging roots to dig deep into the soil for valuable mineral trace elements. These three are normally added in a commercial blend at this time. It is likely that certain other materials will also be in this top dressing. The Champagne

61

soil tends to have a high level of chalk and chalk is a form of limestone. The resulting pH is very high which, as the pH is an inverse ratio, means that the soil is very alkaline, a situation which blocks the ability of the plant to assimilate important elements like iron and manganese. This leads to chlorosis, which in turn hampers the photosynthesis essential to produce sugar in the grape. So such elements will be added to the fertiliser, as well as small amounts of boron, zinc, possibly copper and magnesium, also required to combat chlorosis. Once the fertiliser has been lavished on the soil, then the soil between the rows is ploughed for *buttage* – the piling-up of soil round the base of each vine – making sure that the graft itself is covered over.

This ploughing has a number of functions. The graft, the place where the *vinifera* variety has been joined to the chosen rootstock, is the weakest point in the vine. Thus protecting it against potentially very cold weather by banking up round it is highly sensible, if not essential. Moreover, this process incorporates into the soil any fertiliser that has been scattered, and finally it leaves a trench which can be used for manuring the soil if desired. This is normally done during the very darkest months of December and January.

Such manure tends to be organic. In the days before tractors, it was supplied by the many horses used in the vineyards. When, as a result of mechanisation, this became difficult to obtain, it was replaced by the finely ground contents of the Paris dustbins, known as the *boues de ville*. It was brought in huge sealed containers during the autumn only, according to Patrick Forbes, ground finely because of the danger of broken glass, and left in huge evil-smelling mounds at the edge of the vineyards. Many a visitor to the area has asked about the tiny blue streaks spotted lying among the vines. These are the residue from the plastic bags in which the rubbish was stored before shredding, and is the only element of the *boues* which is definitely not biodegradable.

By the end of the 1970s, Reims itself had sufficient rubbish to obviate transporting the *boues* from Paris, but the use of such manure has been severely checked for a simple economic reason. It has become very expensive of late, since it can now be used in the production of energy, an industry which can pay a far higher price than the growers of grapes.

Today, therefore, there are two main sources of organic matter. The first is simply the spent residue of the winemaking process.

This is the pips, stalks and skins, known as the *marc*, which remains after the pressing has been completed. The other is the 'black gold' of Champagne, which was created over the centuries from the decomposed remains of the ancient forests which once covered the region. Technically known as lignite, a substance somewhere between peat and coal, it occurs in deep minable deposits, particularly on the Montagne de Reims. This lignite is high in carbon, which is absolutely essential to all plant life, and it also contains other much-needed trace elements. These *cendres noirs*, to give the local name, also protect against chlorosis. It says a great deal about the price now being paid for household rubbish that it is now cheaper to mine this lignite, which lies under the tertiary debris left by the two earthquakes.

While any desired manure is spread, the vineyards are gradually cleaned up, with untidy shoots missed during November cut back and the training wires cleared of remaining ties from the previous year. When this is completed, full pruning can start. Timing, however, is crucial, as the weather in this marginal region can be very unreliable.

It is customary to begin the serious pruning as the sap starts to rise in the vine, and the buds start to show signs of development. Anyone who has walked through a vineyard at this time of year knows that a newly pruned vine 'bleeds' – the rising sap spills over before the cut seals – and early-budding varieties, such as Chardonnay, are at a particular risk from unexpected frosts. Indeed, if the choice of pruning time proves wrong it can be extremely expensive. This stage in vineyard management is very much a lottery.

Traditionally pruning begins in the middle of March, as illustrated by an anonymous couplet quoted by Patrick Forbes:

> *Taille tôt ... taille tard*
> *Rien ne vaut la taille mars.**

Nevertheless, late frosts are known at this time, as well as in April or even May. In 1997, for example, early and strong development of the vines apparent at Easter time was severely checked by unseasonably cold weather during the subsequent fortnight.

---

* Roughly translated this rhyme reads: *Pruning early or pruning late,/March's pruning is the best date.*

At the same time as pruning, the framework used for the chosen system is checked and repaired, with posts and wires renewed where necessary. Finally, some time before the end of April, the soil banked up round the vines in November is ploughed back, now covering any manure spread earlier, and the vineyard is ready for the growing cycle.

Once the vine has been pruned, commenced its growth cycle, and been fastened into the training system, the possibility of late frost becomes a real hazard. The traditional method to combat this was by using paraffin burners, known locally as *chaufferettes*, strategically placed among the vines. However, growers who can afford to do so install sprinkler systems with which the vines can be sprayed. To date this is the most effective method of frost protection and is particularly necessary in a cool northerly area where the vines are pruned close to the ground. The need for reflected heat to help with the ripening process equally leads to a far higher risk of (notably late) frost damage. A vine trained 3 metres high is considerably safer than one trained at about 1 metre or less.

The aspersion method requires sprinkling the vines with water from the moment that the temperature drops to about 1°C (34°F) – just above freezing point. So long as the spray continues, and it must do so until the temperature rises to a safe degree, the water freezes around the buds, leaves, or even berries, creating latent heat and so protecting young growth. While this continues, the ice increases on the outside only, but if it ceases the ice will move inwards, destroying any young development. Once the temperature again reaches a safe degree, the spraying can be switched off, the ice melts and the vine returns to normal.

By May it is usual for the vine's growth to have begun in earnest. At this point it is necessary to start spraying against both pests and diseases, and this will continue throughout the growth cycle until about one month before the expected harvest date. Depending on the lie of the land, such treatments may be carried out by hand or, most usually, by tractors fitted with spraying systems or, in some instances, by helicopters. The problem with the latter is that the spray is difficult to contain within a given area.

In such a cool, normally humid climate, spraying against the cryptogamic, or fungal, diseases is essential. But there can be long-term problems. To give just one example, when the first and highly successful anti-rot sprays were introduced, they were used with such enthusiasm that by the middle to late 1980s they had lost their effectiveness; new compounds thereafter contained instructions from the CIVC on their much more sparing use. For the time being, this approach seems to have worked.

Flowering normally takes place from mid-June, although following a late and cold spring this can be as late as early July, and the date of the harvest is usually calculated as being one hundred days after the flowering. The flowering itself is expected between six to eight weeks after the bud burst. The flowers are insignificant in appearance, but the weather at this time is all-important to the size of the vintage. Perfect conditions comprise warmth, dryness and a slight wind. Without these conditions the set may be small, with either the flowers or the tiny green berries dropping off owing to inadequate fertilisation – a condition called *coulure*. Alternatively, bunches may develop with a few large grapes but many more tiny ones, called here *millerandage*, but sometimes known as 'hen and chicken'. Either of these conditions affects the size of the harvest.

From early June, alongside regular spraying, the vine's green growth is thinned and new growth cut back to ensure that the strength of the vine goes into ripening the grapes. Any sterile shoots are removed, but it is essential not to remove too many leaves, since it is the green leaves which, via photosynthesis, use sunlight to manufacture sugar.

Initially, the berries develop size quite rapidly, making seeds, bulk and acids. Then for a short period they appear to stand still, but the seeds are in fact maturing. Then the berry starts its final ripening, about four weeks before the harvest. At this time, known as *véraison*, the green berry will start to show its true pigmentation, the acid levels start to drop and sugar levels develop.

During this ripening period, work continues to keep the weeds clear so that they do not compete with the vine for moisture or food. Gentle summer pruning is carried out, if necessary, until the vintage commences.

The last few weeks before the vintage are nerve-racking for the growers. No matter how great the expectations, how healthy the grapes appear to be, this can all be spoilt by rain at the wrong time, as has happened several times since the 1990 vintage, the last of three great consecutive years.

The vintage normally starts in late September or early October.

There is no fixed date. The state of the grapes dictates the picking, and since 1987 separate dates have been set for each commune.

Champagne always seems very crowded during the three weeks it normally takes to pick the grapes. The vineyards are full of groups of pickers wielding their scissors and often chatting away. One estimate suggests that as many as 60,000 people help pick. This is still a very traditional area and the sights seem to attract a myriad of tourists, even though the weather may be far from ideal for sightseeing.

The bunches are placed carefully in small plastic containers, so that there is no danger of damage to them before pressing. One part of the process, though, has changed. The picking-over of the bunches and removal of poor or rotted grapes, which in the past was done by the older women sitting at the edge of the vineyards with their small scissors, is no more. Improved techniques in both juice-handling and winemaking seem to have rendered *épluchage*, as it is called, redundant. While better handling of the must is certainly a fact, it is difficult to believe that commercial considerations do not play a significant part, especially since a handful of great houses, such as Roederer, do still practise it.

No longer, too, is there the enormous fluctuation in the amount harvested. Since the economic crisis for Champagne in the early 1990s, the maximum yield has been set at 10,200 kilos per hectare. Gone are the days when a harvest could be 15,000 kilos per hectare, as in 1983.

Once picked and placed in the plastic containers containing air holes, the grapes are moved as swiftly as possible to the pressing stations, many of which stand in the vineyards themselves. They are often ugly-looking buildings, but essential for the swift pressing needed to give clean, unoxidised must. They work day and night during the vintage and then fall silent when the last permitted grape has been picked and pressed. Again, the leaves begin to turn in the almost deserted vineyards, and the whole cycle begins again.

Virtue out of Necessity – The Winemaking

Champagne differs from the other great *appellation* wines of France in that it is rarely the product of a single year, apart from specific vintages, or a single vineyard (Krug's Le Mesnil, for example). In essence it is a blended, branded wine known by the name of the maker, the shipper, the retailer or the restaurant, for despite the greatest care and skill in the vineyards, the highly variable climate of this northerly region to a large extent dictates the quality of the wine. Thus the rather dismal, wet summer of 1984 gave a high incidence of bunch rot and low sugar levels, leading to relatively poor quality wines. Yet in the following year, 1985, the beneficent conditions led to fine, well-structured wines with wonderful ripe fruit acidity and great ageing potential. It is for this reason that the Champenois have learnt to blend together wines from several years, so that a standard of quality may be maintained.

Normally, the vintage in Champagne starts one hundred days after flowering and extends over about four weeks, as the three grape varieties will reach maturity at different times in the various areas. Climatic conditions, too, obviously affect the harvest dates. In the last twenty years alone picking has started as early as 1 September in the hot summer of 1976 to as late as 9 October, as it did in 1978 and 1980.

In the weeks building up to the harvest, the grapes are regularly checked for sugar and acid balance, looking for a ripeness that will yield between 10 and 11° alcohol in the base wine, and good strong acidity. Since by law champagne must not exceed 13°, and the second fermentation normally raises the alcohol by about 1.5°, the time of picking is crucial, but in addition recent research into the mousse has shown that 10–11° does give the best foam retention.

During the harvest every effort is made to handle the grapes as gently as possible, since bruising or breaking the skins before pressing will lead to oxidation and can also produce bitter-tasting wines. The entire crop is picked by hand and obviously rotten grapes discarded. The grapes are packed into small plastic containers, which are in turn loaded into bins and taken to the presses.

The press houses are often situated in the vineyards, since speed of pressing after picking is very important, and the shorter the distance the grapes have to travel, the less chance there is of damage.

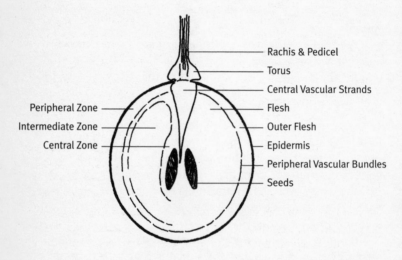

Rachis & Pedicel
Torus
Central Vascular Strands
Peripheral Zone
Flesh
Intermediate Zone
Outer Flesh
Central Zone
Epidermis
Peripheral Vascular Bundles
Seeds

Structure of the grape

Pressing is all-important if the finished wine is to have the delicacy and mousse required. The grape is divided into three main areas. The layer just under the skin, and the central area surrounding the seeds, produce components which, although often highly desirable in still wines, detract from the quality of champagne by inhibiting the formation of the mousse. The skin itself holds waxy substances which also detract from the ability of the wine to foam. The intermediate area, however, about 50 per cent of the grape's volume, is rich in both sugar and tartaric acid, and the objective of the pressing is to obtain as much of the must from this part as possible.

There are three main types of press used: the traditional vertical one which has been developed from the original press designed by Dom Pérignon, called the *pressoir coquart*, and the horizontal screw (Vaslin) and the bladder press (Wilmes or Bucher).

The press most widely used is the vertical *pressoir coquart*. Whether square or round in shape, the bottom half is made from oak and has a series of channels through which the must drains. The grapes are pressed by a wooden flap split in two. The horizontal Vaslin relies on two metal plates at either end of the screw which move slowly towards the centre pressing the grapes, while the pneumatic Wilmes, or Bucher, relies on a gently expanding air or water bag. Traditionally 4,000 kilos of grapes, known as a *marc*, are pressed at one time, but much larger presses, handling two or even three *marcs* together do exist.

Until very recently each *marc* produced 2,666 litres of must, with any remaining juice, the *vin de rebêche*, not being used for champagne but often distilled or sent for vinegar. This 2,666 litres was obtained by three pressings, known as the *cuvée, première taille* and *deuxième taille*. The *cuvée* would be 2,050 litres, equivalent to 10 *pièces* – the traditional champagne barrel of 205 litres. This *cuvée* is the highest quality, with the best sugar and acid content, giving wines with ageing potential. The *première taille* gave 410 litres (2 *pièces*) of juice with more obvious fruit, but less acidity and ageing ability, and finally the *deuxième taille* gave 205 litres of the least quality, low in acid, heavy in fruit, but also often rather herbaceous. Many of the great houses would make their champagne from the *cuvée* only, selling on the *taille* wines.

For many years there was discussion in the area about eliminating use of the *deuxième taille* to protect quality, but during the boom years of the 1980s no action was taken. However, following the collapse of the export markets from 1990 onwards, a decision was taken to reduce the amount of must from a *marc*. From 1992 onwards the *cuvée* remains at 2,050 litres, but the *taille* may produce only 500 litres, and there is no *deuxième taille*. The first 50 litres pressed, which contain any residue of dust and wax from the skins, are no longer treated and then, if clean enough, added back, but have to be discarded. This was the practice of many excellent makers in any case, but it is now mandatory on all

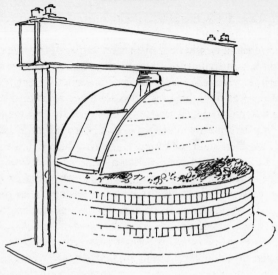

The traditional champagne press

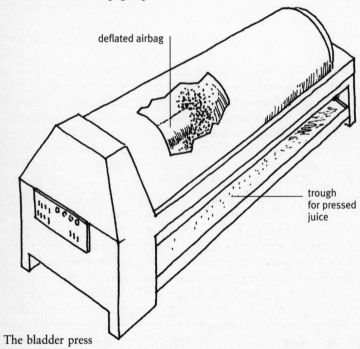

deflated airbag

trough
for pressed
juice

The bladder press

producers. Effectively, therefore, a *marc* now produces 2,500 litres, a reduction of just over 6 per cent.

All the pressings, whether *cuvée* or *taille*, from the different grape varieties and vineyards are kept separate until the blending process begins, after the base wine has been made.

Following pressing, the must has some sulphur dioxide (SO_2) added and is allowed to settle, a process known as *débourbage*. This used to be done by allowing it to fall from the presses into a tank with wooden slats which acted as a sieve, and a few makers still do this. But it is much more usual these days to send the juice through a stainless steel strainer and then keep it cool in a vat for anywhere between eight to twelve hours, after which the clear must is drawn off for the first fermentation. Some establishments use a centrifuge to hasten this process.

If the weather has been poor and the grapes lack sufficient natural sugar to produce the 11.5° alcohol needed, chaptalisation takes place. This process allows cane or beet sugar to be added to the must in order to increase the potential alcohol of the finished wine. Properly used, it is a wonderful aid for winemakers in cool climates, enabling them to achieve a balance in the wine, just as winemakers in hot climates often achieve balance by adding tartaric acid.

The different lots now undergo normal alcoholic fermentation. Once this took place in wooden barrels, the 205-litre *pièces*. Today nearly all first fermentation takes place in stainless steel, although some houses, notably Krug and Alfred Gratien, still use oak, and some others, such as Bollinger, use a mixture of both. Natural yeast is still widely used, but recently there has been a tendency towards inoculation with specific strains of *Saccharomyces cerevisiae*, and occasionally bentonite may be used during the fermentation if it has been a difficult harvest. The temperature is controlled at between 18 and 20°C.

When the fermentation is complete, each vat goes through stringent quality tests to ensure the wine is free from defects. It is then racked off the gross lees into a clean vat where it is held at about 20°C until the malolactic fermentation is complete.

The Malolactic Fermentation

The *malo*, as it is usually called, is a biochemical process which converts the naturally hard malic (apple) acid into the softer lactic (milk) acid and carbon dioxide (CO_2). This process appears to have been first recognised by Dr Müller, of Müller-Thurgau fame, in 1891, but it was Professor Emile Peynaud in Bordeaux who first investigated this phenomenon in depth after the Second World War.

During the ripening period, the malic acid in the grape is reduced. It follows, therefore, that in the cooler areas the grapes, which in most years ripen less fully than those grown in hot areas, will have a higher proportion of this acid than those grown, say, in the Midi or Australia. This will result in a sharp, tart crispness, as found in Granny Smith apples.

As with fermentation, the *malo* is a natural process, being the result of a bacterial attack on the malic acid content of a wine. Three strains of lactic acid bacteria have been identified in natural malolactic fermentations: Pediococcus, *Leuconostos* and Lacto-bacillus. It has been found to occur more easily when the temperature of the cellar is 15°C or more, when minimum amounts of SO_2 have been used, when the newly made wine is still on its lees, which supply the nutrients needed for the bacteria to work, and when the pH levels are between 3.2 and 3.5.

Without these conditions the *malo* is unlikely to start spontaneously. However, today, as with most other winemaking practices, it can be induced, normally using carefully selected strains of Leuconostos, allowing the winemaker to choose whether to encourage or exclude this conversion process.

In simple terms, the *malo* converts 1 gram of malic acid into 0.5 gram of lactic acid, creating some CO_2 in the process, and decreasing the acidity in the wine, increasing the pH by up to 0.2 pH unit. It thus alters the organoleptic perception of the wine, making it less harsh and therefore more attractive for early consumption.

The *malo* has three main effects on the wine. As has been shown, it decreases the fixed acidity, increases microbiological stability, thus lessening the amount of SO_2 needed, and it can, in certain circumstances, increase the flavour complexity early on in the life of the wine. But, on the debit side, it is a process which must be handled very carefully or by-products, not always beneficial, can be created. Examples here would include production of very bitter-tasting substances, and some researchers believe it can also lead to increased levels of hydrogen sulphide (H_2S).

It is often said, and widely believed, that wines which exclude the *malo* gain a longer potential lifespan and added complexity with age. Certainly a case can be made for this with some still white wines from areas of naturally high acidity, such as Alsace and Germany. However, in Champagne this is not necessarily the case. At Pommery the feeling is that the *malo* removes over-high acidity and gives the wine balance, while Moët's Richard Geoffrey, at present responsible for Dom Pérignon, feels strongly that the argument for or against the *malo* is really a question of style.

The Dom Pérignon wines undergo full malolactic fermentation, and can never be accused of being short-lived, simple wines. At Krug, on the other hand, the *malo* is never carried out before the second fermentation in bottle. Interestingly enough, though, Henri Krug believes that the *malo* probably does take place in the bottle, but that the length of time his wines spend on their lees – six years – means that it is complete and finished with long before disgorgement. One of the main arguments for inducing the *malo* before the *prise de mousse* is that this prevents it taking place in the bottle and possibly leading to cloudiness, particularly in wines destined to be sold young.

It may be that the far longer ageing times currently forced on the Champenois by the fall in their home and export markets will lead to a reassessment by some houses of their need for the *malo*. At present, however, according to the Station Œnotechnique de Champagne, about 80 per cent of all wines do undergo it, and the majority of makers see the *malo* as a useful and almost essential part of the winemaking. The advantages appear great – reduction of acidity, increased stability and earlier maturation (and therefore sales) – but it does reduce ageing potential in the wines and, particularly in warm years such as 1976 or 1988 and 1989, acidity can be reduced to the point where it requires adjustment with added tartaric acid. As a generalisation, therefore, for great vintage wines it is normally avoided, and some houses choose to exclude it totally, but most see it as a very useful tool.

The new wine now rests during the winter months, during which it will usually be racked twice, and probably cold-stabilised to remove any excess of potassium bitartrate and thus prevent subsequent precipitation of crystals in the finished wine. In addition, all separate vats are tasted every week so as to decide which style of champagne that particular wine is likely to suit.

In the spring following the vintage, the wines are ready for blending. In the case of a vintage wine, the blend will be from the wines of that year only, while for non-vintage wines the blend will include reserve wines kept from previous years so as to create a 'house' style which never varies. Enormous skill is required when making the blend in the laboratory, and often the ability to do this runs in families. The blend is frequently, though not invariably, made from thirty or forty different wines from various areas. The assemblage should create the house style, particularly in non-vintage wines, and it is very interesting that sometimes, even with the greatest champagnes, the successful blend may not contain the finest still wines, since these can sometimes unbalance the finished product. In other words, the sum of the blending is more important than the individual wines themselves.

Each house guards its blends jealously in order to preserve its own style, but in fact many non-vintage wines are made from approximately one-third of each of the three varieties, although the actual blend will obviously vary according to the conditions of the harvest.

Once the right wines and proportions have been decided, the wines are blended in commercial quantities, following which they will be rested, fined with gelatine combined with tannin, and with bentonite, and then have a final racking. At this point the champagne process proper starts with the addition of the *liqueur de tirage*, prior to bottling for the second fermentation or *prise de mousse*.

The *liqueur de tirage* consists of fine cane sugar dissolved in wine which will be added, together with a selected yeast culture, to the wine. Since it is known that 4 grams per litre of sugar will produce about 1 atmosphere of pressure, then to produce a fully sparkling champagne it is necessary to add 24 grams of sugar per litre of wine to produce 6 atmospheres of pressure and also to raise the alcoholic content by about 1.5 percentage by volume. As a side note, it has been found that over 28 grams per litre most bottles will break. Equally, to make the more gently sparkling champagne, previously known as *crémant* (although this term ceased to be legal in Champagne on 31 August 1994), about 14 grams per litre needs to be added. This syrup and yeast is then added to the blended wine in a tank and mixed in. Additionally an agent, such as bentonite, is usually added to assist with the subsequent *remuage* since it helps to prevent yeast sticking too firmly to the side of the bottle.

The wine is now bottled, and a *bidule* (a small plastic insert to prevent contact with the metal cap) and crown cap seal each bottle. Originally cork was used at this point, but today this is comparatively rare and usually used only for very special wines which will take long ageing, since it has been shown that wines with the crown cap age more swiftly than those with cork closures. The filled bottles are then taken down to the cool cellars and left lying horizontally, *sur lattes*, in a temperature that remains stable at about 10°C for the second fermentation. The slower and cooler this second fermentation, the finer the resulting wine when it is well matured, and certainly the finer the bubbles. Once the fermentation is complete the wine rests on its lees for a period. The law now stipulates fifteen months in cellar for non-vintage wines and three years for vintage wines. After a period of about eight months after bottling, the dead yeast cells begin to degrade and break down. This process, called yeast autolysis, releases volatile aromas, amino acids and proteins which give the special 'champagne' aromas and flavours. It therefore follows that the longer the wine remains in contact with the yeast, the more developed this character becomes, and many makers do in fact leave even their non-vintage wines on the lees for about three years. Often during this ageing period the wines are shaken and restacked (*poignetage*) with the objective of making the sediment less sticky.

The next step is to move the yeast sediment on to the cap in preparation for its removal. Today this may be done by hand or mechanically. If the classic hand method is used, the bottles are placed in *pupitres*, the wooden racks said to have been developed by Veuve Cliquot. The bottles are shaken to loosen the sediment and placed in the racks neck down and at an angle of about 35°, where they are then left for about three weeks to settle before *remuage*, or riddling, proper takes place.

Hand *remuage* is a great art, and even today, when it is claimed that about 70 per cent of all champagne goes through mechanical *remuage*, most houses do keep some *remueurs* even if only for their finest products. The bottles are turned about one-eighth off the centre each day, being slightly shaken in the process, and gradually being inclined towards the vertical as the deposit slides down towards the neck. A *remueur* can handle 40–50,000 bottles a day. This activity often leaves the *remueur* with arthritic wrists, but, despite this, its practitioners clearly take pride in their work and they are among the highest-paid workers in the champagne industry. And at this stage it is possible to see clearly the difference the addition of some form of riddling aid at bottling makes. If the traditional gelatin and tannin were used – rarely done now as it increases ageing time – the deposit tended to stick and *remuage* was a difficult task and not suitable for mechanical systems. With the addition of bentonite, the deposit moves much more easily, but the Station Œnotechnique has produced a blend of bentonite and alginates which prevents the deposit sticking to the glass and is very suitable for automatic systems.

The mechanical systems vary from a hand-operated hexagonal basket, known as *Champarex* and used by many small makers, to large automatic systems such as the *gyropalette* which holds 504 bottles and can complete *remuage* in about one week. This of course allows for a far greater amount of *remuage*, since the hand system may take up to eight to ten weeks to complete, depending on the wine.

Once the deposit is safely in the neck of the bottle, the wine may proceed to disgorgement immediately, but often special champagnes are kept in the cellars for years of extra maturation, stacked neck to punt, *sur pointes*.

Dégorgement is the removal of the deposit. Just as with *remuage*, it may be done by hand, but this is becoming rarer as the automatic process is efficient and gives excellent results, whereas if *dégorgement* by hand is carried out improperly, there can be swift deterioration of the wine. But whichever method is chosen, the bottle will almost certainly first pass through the freezing brine process. The neck only will be placed into a salt solution at −30°C. The wine at the neck is frozen into a slushy pellet and this freezing process also temporarily reduces the pressure inside the bottle by a small amount. If it is then disgorged manually, the bottle will be gradually moved towards upright and the opener placed at the cap. The moment the rising bubbles reach the ice plug the cap is removed, the plug flies out under the CO_2 pressure and a thumb is placed over the top until the bottle is placed on the machine which adds the *dosage*. Far more probably today, the bottle will be placed on a machine which removes the cap and allows the ice plug to be ejected before moving the bottle to the *dosage* machine.

The *dosage*, or *liqueur d'expédition*, is a mixture of wine and sugar added to balance the acidity of the now very dry wine or to give the wine a degree of sweetness, if it is so desired. The *dosage* is made by adding the desired proportion of sugar (see table on page 80), preferably to wine of the same blend as that to be disgorged. It is mixed a few weeks earlier to ensure that no reaction takes place, and usually a tiny amount of SO_2 is added to protect against oxidation. In past times occasionally a small amount of cognac was added if the wine was low in alcohol, but today this practice has almost entirely vanished.

The *dosage* machine has three separate operations. It removes a little wine, adds the liqueur and then adds back some of the wine removed to give a proper fill height. Finally the wine is corked, wired and shaken to make sure that the *dosage* is well mixed in. After this it is rested for a legal minimum of one month, but often for longer, before the bottles are rinsed, dried, polished and finally receive their foil and label when they are ready for packing and shipment.

Chacun à son gout

═══════════

It is surprising how many people outside the wine trade believe that champagne is a single product, namely fizzy wine, and that one glass is much the same as another, while they might well be happy arguing for the merits of, say, Australian Cabernet Sauvignon compared to Chilean or Californian styles. It seems that the moment a mousse is developed, it is regarded not so much as a wine per se, but as a somewhat frivolous drink, and this blinds people to the range of wines that can be produced.

To begin at the beginning, every maker produces a non-vintage wine, relying on the house blend and the final *dosage* to establish a recognisable house style. The differences are considerable.

Then they will probably also make a vintage wine in the good years, possibly a *blanc de blancs* and a *rosé* as well. In addition, the house might produce a *blanc de noirs*, a style with a lower pressure (once, but no longer, termed *crémant*) and a *cuvée de prestige*. These are all sparkling wines. Over and above this come the still wines or Côteaux Champenois and two other drinks, *ratafia* and *eau-de-vie*. In short, the region can and does produce a wide range of styles – something for everyone.

Non-vintage wine is by far the largest single category in Champagne and, contrary to the public's perception, most houses do regard this as their flagship wine in that it represents their unique style. As the name suggests, this is the result of blending wines of a particular year with those from previous years, known as reserve wines. In any vintage, a percentage of the still wines made may be kept for subsequent use. It is this clever blending between vintages, vineyard areas and grape varieties that produces the house style.

The law requires a fifteen-month ageing period from bottling for the second fermentation before sale. This used to be twelve months and there is talk of, when possible, raising this to an eighteen-month period, which would probably be wise since the developing sparkling-wine-producing countries such as Australia and the USA (notably California and Oregon) believe in a minimum two-and-a-half-year period for their high-quality production.

The non-vintage wines are variously estimated to account for between 80 and 90 per cent of the total production. This is a difficult figure to quantify, since in tremendously good years, such as 1996, a higher than usual proportion will be made as vintage or even *cuvée de prestige*, whereas in difficult years, like 1992 and 1993, the opposite happens. But there is no doubt that these days most producers, whether from the disbanded Grandes Marques or the small village grower or co-operative, regard non-vintage wines as commercially the most important.

It is also often forgotten that NV wines do not have to be *brut* in style. There are, even today, varying degrees of sweetness permitted. The following list gives, in grams of sugar per litre of wine in the *dosage* (*liqueur d'expédition*), the amount legally allowed in each style. Here it has to be admitted that many of the sweeter styles do need to be specially ordered, as the general market prefers the dry. The preference of Queen Elizabeth, the Queen Mother, for a less dry style is believed, for example, to have led to the reintroduction of the Pol Roger Demi-Sec on to the UK market.

The terms *brut sauvage*, *brut zéro*, and other such labels like *non-dosage*, *sans sucre* or even *ultra brut* (in the case of the marvellous Laurent-Perrier product), mean that no sugar whatsoever has been added to the *dosage*. These wines do need extra ageing and can be wonderful, although slightly green and tart if drunk too young.

Brut is the expected style on this market, in which there will be no more than 15 grams of sugar per litre in the finished wine after addition of the *dosage* wine. Many growers add as little as between 4 and 7 grams, but will change the amount according to the wine's need. Thus NV wine from a blend of thinner or greener years will require maybe 12–14 grams, while those from richer years far less.

The following two terms can be slightly misleading to the English speaker. *Sec* is understood to mean 'dry', yet wines from Champagne labelled as either *extra sec* (containing after the *dosage* between 12 and 20 grams of sugar) or *sec* (between 17 and 35 grams), depending on the palate of the consumer, can feel anything from dry to medium sweet.

Demi-sec, translated as medium dry, would certainly be regarded by most as a sweet style, the *dosage* containing between 35 and 50 grams of sugar per litre, while the genuinely sweet styles (*doux*) have over 50 grams per litre in the finished wine. Just as beauty lies in the eyes of the beholder, so sweetness levels are in the taste of the consumer. One person's medium dry is another person's medium to sweet. The other essential factor is the balance of the individual wines. For example, if acidity, and also fruit and alcoholic weight, is high, then *dosage*, even at the *brut* level, can be correspondingly high without affecting the taste.

It is important also to remember that the *dosage* can vary according to fashion in the country of export. Thus the *dosage* for the UK market may well contain a different proportion of sugar compared to the French, for example, or the US – a fact which was noted by Henry Vizetelly as early as 1882.

Extra Brut	less than 6 grams per litre
Brut	less than 15 grams per litre
Extra Sec	12–20 grams per litre
Sec	17–35 grams per litre
Demi-Sec	35–50 grams per litre
Doux	over 50 grams per litre

Vintage champagne is now highly sought after, yet any scrutiny of wine lists during the late 1970s will show that most merchants relied on a large selection of non-vintage wines with just one or two vintages listed. In the early days, before the idea of reserve wines surfaced, every champagne had to be a vintage. It appears to have been the 1874 dry wine, imported into the UK, that set the fashion for special vintage years, although there are earlier recorded ones. Apparently, following the 1939–45 war, the monarchy felt that austerity should be followed, and vintage champagne at banquets, receptions, etc, was replaced by non-vintage which then, of course, became the normal choice. It was only during the mid- to late 1970s that the balance swung back, although most people most of the time still buy non-vintage.

The base wine for a vintage champagne is required by law to achieve a higher natural level of alcohol than a non-vintage (at least 1 per cent higher) before chaptalisation. In fact, both tend to have between 12 and 12.5° in the final bottle. The law requires considerably more ageing. At least three years from bottling for the second fermentation is needed, but in practice many wines, particularly from great houses, will have much greater ageing. As opposed to non-vintage, every drop in the bottle has to come from the same year. Whereas the non-vintage of any producer should show the house style, the vintage wine should really show the conditions of the year overlying it.

The law further requires that, however brilliant the vintage, by no means all the wines can be declared as such; 20 per cent at the very minimum *must* be kept in reserve to become part of subsequent NV wines.

Traditionally, only the very best years were declared by the houses, but sadly, during the massive expansion of the champagne market in the 1980s, many makers jumped on to the vintage bandwagon and produced lightweight, acidic and over-dosed wines for the seemingly voracious market, thus rendering the reputation of great champagnes a great deal of harm. The disappointing harvests of the early 1990s have somewhat rectified this situation. Between the rich 1990s and the potentially rather elegant 1995s there was little to excite the market, but the early indications of the 1996 wines suggest a remarkable vintage which will thankfully not be available until after the Millennium. This will give it a chance to age quietly and show its quality in due time.

Blanc de blancs wines are a specific style – lighter, crisp and made from Chardonnay vines only. Until 1980, there were three other varieties permitted – Pinot Blanc Vrai, Petit Meslier and Arbanne – but no longer. Most, obviously, come from the Côte des Blancs, but this is not necessarily always the case since every area does grow some Chardonnay. Thus, though relatively rare, *blanc de blancs* can be found from the Aube, the Côte de Sézanne and the Vallée de la Marne. Usually the lightest and freshest style, many people find their way into enjoying champagne through the *blanc de blancs* route, and for many it remains their favourite. Certainly a splendid aperitif wine, it is noticeable that, with bottle age, some can and do develop into big, long-lived wines of great fruit and character. This may well have everything to do with the sourcing of the fruit. At Pommery, Ruinart and Taittinger the winemakers are convinced that Chardonnay from the Montagne de Reims gives an entirely different style of wine, and fruit from this area is much sought after.

A wine labelled *blanc de noirs* is exactly that: a white wine made from the black grapes only. This is a style which has been very much out of fashion until recently, but with the rapidly growing interest in pairing wine with food, however, the *blanc de noirs* is making a comeback. Its problem, for champagne purists, is that all too often the wines, made from Pinot Noir, Pinot Meunier or a blend of the two, can be almost over-fruity and rather heavy or clumsy, lacking the complexity and elegance given by the blend with Chardonnay. But this very defect, if it is one, makes these wines sometimes more suitable for drinking with a meal, especially rich dishes.

Undoubtedly the most famous of all the *blanc de noirs* wines is the Bollinger Vieilles Vignes Françaises, about which more later. However, many small growers marketing their own wines, often at the cellar door, do have little choice in the style they make, since only very rarely are they able to purchase grapes on the market. Thus a vigneron whose vineyard grows only black grapes will have no choice in the matter, but it is rare for any champagne to declare *blanc de noirs* on the label. It is interesting today, therefore, to see that some major British supermarkets are offering bottles clearly labelled as such.

Pink, or *rosé*, champagne has been a wine whose popularity has gone in cycles. Enormously popular during the Edwardian era, and then again in the late 1940s and early 1950s, it nearly disappeared until the boom period of the 1980s. Looking at its popularity peaks and troughs, it seems fair to say that whenever either heights of prosperity, frivolity, or both, dominate the social scene, then pink fizz will become the drink.

The house of Clicquot appears to have produced the first commercially made *rosé* champagne, claiming 1777 for its origin. It was not always popular. Ever since then, dedicated drinkers of white champagne have tended to despise it. This is not entirely fair. Certainly there are, and have been, many poor-quality pink wines made during the boom times, but then this has also applied to any champagne. A fine *rosé* should show a distinctive red-grape influence both in aroma and taste. A good test is to smell and taste the wine with the eyes closed, and preferably against a standard wine, when this Pinot character should show though. It is a pity that not all *rosé* wines can do this. All too often they seem to rely on the attractive appearance, pink in the glass and with a white mousse on the surface.

Within the European Union there is only one generally permitted way to make pink wine. The colour has to be extracted from the skins. The exact method can vary: it might simply come from pressing black grapes sufficiently hard for some pink tinges to be transferred to the juice; or allowing a short maceration on the skins before pressing and allowing fermentation to continue as for white wines; equally it may be produced by 'bleeding' (*saignée*), a method which can be particularly useful in cool northern climates where the pigmentation in the skins may be low. Some of the fermenting must is drawn off when a sufficient level of colour has been achieved, thus reducing the ratio of juice to skins and intensifying the colour in the remaining must. What is not allowed, however, is the blending of red and white wine to produce a pink one – except in Champagne. Here blending is permitted under both the AOC and European law because it had been a long-standing traditional practice in the region.

Most pink champagne is indeed produced by blending, although some houses, notably Laurent-Perrier, do produce a genuinely *rosé* still wine before the *prise de mousse*. Between 10 and 20 per cent of the wine in the *cuvée* before bottling may be still red wine produced in Champagne, but one of the problems is frequently the destabilisation of colour which can take place during the second fermentation. There is, therefore, no standard colour for these wines, which can vary from almost white to occasionally almost iridescent shades of pink. One small grower even tried to take advantage of the vogue for blush wines when showing his exceedingly pale pink champagne. Because of this, it is permitted to use red wine also in the *liqueur d'expédition*. This, however, is a hotly debated issue, with many believing that in some way this is cheating.

The highest-quality wines are sometimes bottled and sold as *cuvées de prestige*. Two examples immediately leap to mind: Roederer Cristal and Moët's Dom Pérignon. The former, originally made specifically for the Tsar of Russia and the Imperial Court, may lay claim to be the oldest, but as far as commercial availability for the whole champagne market is concerned, Dom Pérignon takes that honour. Since the success of these two brands, many other houses have produced such wines, among the best-known being

Comtes de Champagne from Taittinger, Perrier-Jouët's Belle Époque, with its beautiful art nouveau bottle, and Dom Ruinart.

Some of these wines are made as vintage wines. Others, like Laurent-Perrier's Cuvée Grand Siècle, are a blend of two or three high-quality years. Often, too, they are made from grapes sourced from *grand cru* sites only, or from the vineyards owned by the house concerned, and not brought in. Inevitably they are very expensive, but do represent a quality which the maker believes to be the very best.

There is, or used to be, one other style. Until 1 September 1994, *crémant* was a legal term in Champagne. Essentially, this was an old style well known in the eighteenth and nineteenth centuries when, frequently, it was preferred to fully sparkling wines. The literal translation is 'creaming', referring to the fact that it is gentler in the mouth because of a lower atmospheric pressure, something in the region of a minimum of 3.6 atmospheres, rather than between 5 and 6. This lighter mousse is arrived at simply by adding less sugar to the *cuvée* at the bottling stage, before the *prise de mousse*. For fully sparkling wine, the amount is 22–24 grams per litre; for the lower atmosphere it is 12–14 grams. The most famous commercial *crémant* wine was probably Mumm's Crémant de Cramant, today bottled under the more prosaic name of Mumm de Cramant. Once regarded by connoisseurs as a much superior style, these wines are still made by a few producers. Other noted makers include Besserat de Bellefont and Alfred Gratien.

The term *crémant* now applies to other French regions using the same method as Champagne for their sparkling wines – Alsace and Burgundy, for example – and this has led to considerable confusion. Outside Champagne, the term does not necessarily imply a lower pressure.

As the demand for sparkling champagne grew, so that for the still wines of the region fell away, and from 1953 they were known as *vin nature de Champagne*, which in 1974 became Coteaux Champenois. The *appellation* allows for this still wine to be red, white or *rosé*.

Very little Coteaux Champenois actually appears on the market, and certainly not for export. The demand recently has been for the sparkling wine, and with the now restricted yield the still wines have to come from the same total *rendement* (the permitted yield of grapes per hectare), so naturally wine production goes where the market is. Additionally, these still wines are expensive to buy and not of any great intrinsic quality. According to Tom Stevenson, many makers simply regard them as a form of extra reserve wines.

The area of production, grapes grown, methods of pruning and training are, of course, all identical to those used for sparkling wine, but the main drawback to their production is climatic. For a great sparkling wine, a thin, highly acidic base wine is perfect. This is not the case for still wines, and many of the white Coteaux Champenois are somewhat thin and acid. Two that can be different, especially from better vintages, and are worth seeking out are Moët & Chandon's Saran, and the Chardonnay produced by Ruinart.

Curiously enough, in hot vintages the red wines can be much more interesting. Those from the villages of Bouzy, Aÿ and Cumières particularly so. Most good makers will make this only in warm vintages, when the wine can be surprisingly deep in colour. Laurent-Perrier make a confusingly named but fruity Pinot Franc; Barancourt, a good Bouzy Rouge.

Although permitted by the AOC, little *rosé* Coteaux Champenois is seen, but another *rosé* with its own *appellation* is made within Champagne. Rosé des Riceys is worth a mention here. Grown in the Aube, it is not a champagne at all. As its name suggests, the vineyards are situated in the commune of Les Riceys. The grape is Pinot Noir, and in a good year the colour can be surprisingly deep, more like an Italian *cerasuolo* than a light northern *rosé*. A wine of some antiquity, it is expensive but certainly worth trying.

Champagne also produces various *eaux-de-vie*, or brandies, of two major types. That made from the skins, stalks and pips which remain after the pressing is finished is called *marc*. Most wine-producing regions make a *marc* – it is not confined to Champagne, although when made there from the residue of grapes intended for the AOC wines, it bears the *appellation* 'Eau-de-vie de Marc de Champagne'. A minimum strength of 40° alcohol is required and, like all other *marcs*, it is very fiery in the mouth.

This type of brandy is made by adding water to the spent pressing, which will have enough sugar left to enable a coarse, low-strength wine to be made, which is then distilled. In past days, *marc* was frequently supplied to the vigorous pruning force in cold weather as part of their pay.

The other type of *eau-de-vie* is much finer. It is a distillation of wine made from AOC grapes and originally intended for champagne, but not considered good enough, or from the *vin de rebêche* or even wine left after racking. Although its full *appellation* is 'Eau-de-vie de vin de la Marne Réglementée', in practice it is known as Fine Marne.

The houses are not permitted to carry out their own distillation process. Everything intended for this process must be delivered to one of the authorised distilleries. Afterwards, any distillate required for sale is returned to the source of the raw material where it will be aged, bottled and labelled.

The final product made is ratafia,* a drink once thought suitable for children. The name is said to have derived from the drink shared by the signatories to any form of legal contract – *rata fiat* in Latin. In theory, it can be white, red or *rosé*, and today it is made as a *mistelle*, where unfermented grape juice is blended with high-strength grape spirit, the level of alcohol preventing any fermentation. It is then aged, occasionally in wood but far more often in vat, before being bottled at a minimum strength of 18 per cent.

---

* Some confusion exists over the term 'ratafia', which in previous centuries was frequently a word used for non-alcoholic fruit cordials – hence Mrs Beeton's comment that it was suitable for children. There is even uncertainty over the origin of the word. Although commonly believed to have come from the Latin '*rata*' and '*fiat*', meaning in legal terms that the deal had been ratified, after which the parties to the deal had to share a drink, Walter Skeat in his *Concise Dictionary of English Etymology* states that it comes from the Malay 'araq tafia'.

12

The Champagne Trade

The nineteenth century, which saw the evolution of the champagne method, also witnessed an expansion of the trade. Merchant houses began to proliferate, a surprisingly large number with Germanic names, such as Bollinger, Deutz, Heidsieck, Krug and Mumm, following in the footsteps of houses which had become successful during Napoleonic times, notably Moët, Clicquot, Ruinart and Jacquesson. There is an interesting reason for the sudden German influx. By 1845 a merchant called Max Sutaine was commenting on the fact that the unwillingness of the French to study other languages created the need to employ young, language-gifted German clerks, who would learn the business then set up on their own.

Certainly, there seems to be a pattern. Jacques Bollinger came from Württemberg, began by selling champagne in Germany and was asked to run a company selling the wines of the Comte de Villermont – not under the family name, which would be disgraced by association with commerce, but under his own. Bollinger subsequently married the Comte's daughter. In turn, two of M. Bollinger's German clerks founded Deutz & Gelderman. Johann-Josef Krug from Mainz worked with Jacquesson & Fils until his marriage to his employer's English sister-in-law, after which he left to start Krug.

In spite of the growth in the number of merchants, the French market developed slowly, moving from the production of just over 2 million to just under 3 million bottles in the fifty years from 1840 to 1890. It was not until 1913 that demand rose strongly, reaching about 10.5 million bottles. The expanding wine trade looked to the export markets, which included Britain and Germany (as today), the United States and Tsarist Russia, where champagne was much appreciated.

One of the first to understand the possibilities of the export market was the first of the great ladies of champagne, and the area has produced many of them: the Veuve Clicquot. To her, and her business associate M. Bohne, Russia was a promising market, and by 1806 M. Bohne was sending back reports. Despite the obvious difficulties created by the Napoleonic Wars, the trade continued and the name of Veuve Clicquot champagne was famous. Indeed, in 1811 Charles-Henri Heidsieck arrived to test the market but made no headway. It almost became a Clicquot monopoly, so much so that in 1814 the house broke the Allies' blockade to send the 1811 vintage, all of which was sold before it ever reached St Petersburg. Of all the other merchant houses endeavouring to tackle the Russian market, only Louis Roederer was to have a major success which eventually led to the creation of Cristal especially for Tsar Alexander III.

By 1815, with the coming of peace, the champagne makers needed to start looking for export markets. The domestic market in their still highly prized red wines faded, as the coming of better, cheaper communications opened the routes for red wines from further south. Little by little, markets were opened up in such faraway places as the United States, South America and Cuba, as well as in Switzerland, Italy and Scandinavia, with considerable success, between them taking about 70 per cent of production.

This growing market, however, caused serious problems at the end of the century which had seen so many houses established and great technical advances, and produced some of the legendary figures of Champagne. Jean-Rémy Moët's friendship with Napoleon brought imperial favour, thereby allowing the foundations of the firm's future to be laid, but he also maintained good trading relationships with many of the Allies. Then there was Champagne Charlie, Charles-Camille Heidsieck, and his many visits to America, where he indulged not only in shooting parties and an amazing lifestyle, but on one occasion was mistaken for a Confederate spy and lodged in a Yankee gaol. Eugène Mercier was another great showman, building the biggest cask in the world at that time. It was taken to Paris for the 1889 Exhibition with considerable difficulty, dragged by a team of twenty-four white oxen, while in 1900 a huge balloon with sampling facilities broke from its tether in the Champ-de-Mars and landed its unwitting passengers, with the wine, in Alsace! Even in the champagne business, few characters of this ilk remain.

Phylloxera brought serious problems to the rapidly developing market and, as a result of bureaucratic ineptness in publishing a set of completely inaccurate export figures in 1882, the forerunner of the Syndicat des Grandes Marques was founded to defend the good name of Champagne. It represented the houses and was formed two years before the repeal of an old law, passed during the 1789 Revolutionary period, forbidding such associations. In its early days, the Syndicat acted swiftly and strongly in matters of fraud, but then membership began to decline and in 1912 an alternative was formed by other houses. Eventually, at the end of the Second World War, both syndicates formed a union but kept their distinct identities.

The early part of the twentieth century witnessed disastrous harvests and the vicious riots of 1911. Amazingly, sales had continued to rise in spite of everything, but another catastrophe lay ahead. In the early autumn of 1914 the Germans invaded France, striking through the Marne Valley, and on 3 September Reims fell. Three days later, Epernay was also in German hands. The occupation lasted for only ten days, but a fierce two-day battle was fought in vineyards bearing a heavy crop of ripening fruit. By 13 September, both Reims and Epernay had been retaken, but the front line remained in the district, running along the base of the Montagne de Reims. Four years of bloody fighting ensued and the front hardly moved one hundred yards either way.

Reims itself was subjected to heavy bombardment for most of that period. Great damage was done to the mediaeval cathedral, sheltering refugees at the time, and the fine roof was destroyed. Today, it has been restored with the help of Rothschild money, and the new roof is open to visitors. It appears to be made of wood, like the original, but is in fact concrete. The Palais de Tau next door has a permanent and moving exhibition about the damage sustained during the First World War.

Against all the odds, the local people brought in the 1914 vintage and worked the vineyards, although many, mainly women and children, were wounded or killed doing so. Weary of the incessant bombardment, the citizens of Reims took to the cellars. When heated, these were reasonably comfortable and certainly bombproof. Visitors walking round the Pommery cellars are shown the galleries used, for example, as a hospital. Nevertheless, by the war's end, Reims had been destroyed.

It was rebuilt surprisingly quickly. The Hotel de la Paix in the rue Buirette, used extensively by trade visitors to the city, was the first hotel to reopen in the move towards normality. But peacetime brought its own problems, including the collapse of many carefully cultivated markets. First was Russia, swept away by the Revolution of 1917. Ten per cent of the total export market disappeared and no outstanding bills incurred by the Tsar and his court were paid by the new government. Germany was bankrupt, as was the old Austro-Hungarian empire. Furthermore, the world was suddenly in the grips of a powerful anti-alcohol lobby. This had been noted by the Syndicat before the war, but now it became a political reality. The Scandinavian countries restricted alcohol by a combination of powerful state monopolies and high taxation. Following the Volstead Act, America banned alcohol. Canada soon followed; other states moved towards the monopoly system of control. Britain raised its taxes.

The seriousness of the situation is shown by the figures. In 1913, all sales had totalled nearly 39 million bottles. This was not matched again until the mid-1950s. In one way the collapse of the markets created a breathing space. Major replanting had barely begun before the war, since the phylloxera had moved slowly through the vineyards, and even of those in production, many had been fought over, damaging and destroying the vines. There was no way that the Champenois could have met the requirements of a strong market. Indeed, it was not until the end of the 1920s that the replanted vineyards amounted to 8,000 hectares of regular rows of grafted vines, but then came another major setback. With the area now finally delimited, and the three grape varieties Chardonnay, Pinot Noir and Pinot Meunier enshrined in law, the Great Depression arrived.

The total collapse of the export markets in the early 1930s had one important result for the champagne industry. Deprived of their carefully nurtured outlets (in 1932, for example, there were practically no sales at all), many houses turned their attention to the domestic market with very considerable success. By 1935, sales in France were approximately three bottles for every one exported, a situation which remains more or less the same today. Not that this was a tremendous help at the time. The cellars were heavily stocked, production had been rising while sales slumped, so when the bountiful and high-quality 1934 vintage arrived, most houses already had five years' supply in hand.

Many houses neither could nor would buy the grapes. The price per kilo slumped to an all-time low of 50 centimes. A handful of growers with sufficiently large holdings did invest in equipment and started making their own wine; but many of the grapes remained on the vines, not worth the labour or cost of picking. At the same time, a large number of growers unable to afford such investment began to group together, thus beginning the region's co-operative movement. Drastic action was needed, and in September 1935 a commission comprising representatives of the Ministry of Agriculture, local growers and champagne houses was set up by decree. It soon became known as the Commission of Châlons, where the meetings were held. It tightened regulations generally, reduced the amount of production per hectare, established a juice-extract ratio of 100 litres to 150 kilos of grapes (which remained until the most recent crisis), and insisted on a minimum one year in bottle before sale. These regulations were presented to the industry as protecting local tradition, but although designed to uphold and improve the quality of the wines, they did nothing to help the grape-growers who were again in a parlous state.

One man did recognise that there was a serious long-term problem to be solved. The growers of the raw material needed to be assured that they could earn a living, which would prevent the pitch of desperation reaching such that the growers would switch their holdings to other crops. Robert-Jean de Vogüé, known to his contemporaries as the Red Marquis, hardly had the background of a revolutionary. Distantly related to the Moët family, he initially trained as a soldier, passing out from the Ecole de Guerre, the staff college. His family, though, did have a large interest in Moët & Chandon, and when their market share slipped badly during the early 1930s he joined the firm. He was not a great lover of champagne – it is said he preferred Scotch – but nonetheless he was the individual mainly responsible for Moët's great *cuvée de prestige*, Dom Pérignon, launched in 1935.

In that same year, M. de Vogüé appalled a number of his fellow merchants by proposing at a meeting in Châlons that the price paid for grapes be raised substantially to provide the growers with a proper income. This revolutionary suggestion eventually won the day, though not before M. de Vogüé was dubbed a traitor by some – hence his nickname.

Time was to prove him right. The Depression was retreating, the domestic market was strong, and the level of exports was again rising, helped along by the repeal of the Volstead Act. Prohibition no longer ruled America. Recovery was apparently on its way, only to be halted by the arrival in May 1940 of German troops to occupy the region, where they remained until August 1944.

This time Champagne was spared the appalling physical bombardment of 1914–18, and the period known as the phony war did give the Champenois time to prepare themselves. Some stocks were hidden to preserve them from looting, those Champenois wishing to avoid German occupation had time to leave, while others who chose to stay had prepared small resistance cells.

In one respect, the winemakers were lucky. This time the Germans appointed a commandant for the region with special powers to control the wine industry. He was a wine-grower himself, by name of Kläbisch, and his title was *Weinführer*. Additionally, the Vichy government dissolved the, by now, ineffectual Commission of Châlons and replaced it with a body to be known as the Bureau National de Répartition des Vins de Champagne. In theory it had considerable powers; but Robert-Jean de Vogüé and a man named Maurice Doyard, from Vertus, who had been a powerful influence for the growers during the previous years, believed that this body would also prove ineffectual. They succeeded in convincing the German authorities, since the efficient and highly organised Germans would appreciate dealing with a body which had real power. Thus in the April of 1941 the Bureau National was replaced by the Comité Interprofessionnel du Vin de Champagne, still known today as CIVC. The idea disseminated by de Vogüé and Doyard that the occupying authorities would find it far easier to manage the wine industry if they had to deal with one controlling body had won the argument.

The new Comité was empowered to regulate every aspect of the industry from viticulture through production to trade, and to hold a balance between all parties involved, as well as to intervene in the market in times of shortfall or surplus. Right from the beginning it worked well, very much because of the personal dedication of M. de Vogüé, who resigned from Moët & Chandon to head the organisation. All decisions were taken by an equal number of growers' and makers' representatives, neither side holding a commercial advantage in the voting. It would therefore have seemed a most dreadful blow to the region when news leaked out that M. de Vogüé plus his able assistant, Claude Fourmon, and their interpreter had been arrested by order of the Gestapo while at a regular meeting on behalf of the CIVC with the *Weinführer*. This was late in 1942, and in spite of enemy occupation a wave of revolt spread through the district when it was further known that de Vogüé had been condemned to death. Protesters were fined heavily, but a point had been made and the sentence was deferred, probably, according to Patrick Forbes, because by now all available troop units were required on the Russian front and civil unrest in France would mean deploying extra forces there. Thus Robert-Jean de Vogüé and Claude Fourmon spent the remainder of the war in concentration camps.

They were by no means the only people from Champagne to suffer this fate. The history of the Resistance in this area includes the death of the head of Piper-Heidsieck, the Marquis d'Aulan, while fighting, and the deportation of Bertrand de Vogüé of Veuve Clicquot, as well as those of leading growers. Both Moët & Chandon and Piper-Heidsieck were heavily fined and taken over by German management, in Moët's case because the cellars were the headquarters of a Resistance group. Many ordinary workers in the trade, and many railway workers who were in a perfect position to sabotage troop movements, were also involved, but so successful had been the secrecy that most Champenois were amazed to discover the extent after liberation by the American 3rd Army under General Patton on 28 August 1944. In honour of this event, fortunately swift and unexpected enough to prevent the blowing-up of the cellars ordered by Himmler, the route taken by the Americans is marked by a series of small *bornes* slightly reminiscent of the Daleks in shape, some of which are now being renewed.

At the end of the war, the CIVC was not unnaturally regarded with some suspicion, as it had been formed under the Vichy government, so the institution was placed under the control of an appointee of the government, although it continued to operate as before. Its functions are still as laid out in the original decree of 12 April 1941:

It is the function of this Committee to ensure harmonious relations between vine-growers and merchants, to manage their common interests in the economic, technical and social spheres, and to protect the prosperity of the interprofession, as well as perpetuating champagne wine, and it is a semi-public organisation run by a Commissioner, assisted by the President of the 'Syndicat Général des Vignerons' and the President of the 'Union des Syndicats du Commerce'.

It is administered by a Consultative Committee made up of six vine-growers and six merchants elected by their members. Its principal activities involve:

The regularization of relations between the vine-growers who are also grape-sellers and the purchasing merchants (fixing of prices, distribution of the harvest, the setting-up of pressing and storage facilities, etc.).

The improvement of vine-growing techniques and oenological techniques (research and experimentation, combating pests, frost, hail and vinification hazards, professional training, promoting quality, stamping out fraud, etc.).

The protection and development of the Champagne market in general (documentation, market studies, supply of certificates of origin, informing and educating the public, educating retailers, public relations, defending the appellation Champagne in the courts, etc.).

To cover the cost of its activities, the CIVC derives a budget from levies paid by the vine-growers on their harvests and by the Champagne houses on their bottle sales, as well as from special taxes.

The CIVC relies on the representative bodies of the merchants and vine-growers, from whom it obtains its funds, works closely with the wine agents, the sales agents and the ancillary industries, and has regulatory powers. It is an intermediate structure between the private and public sectors. It is the point at which the sometimes divergent interests of one group or the other coalesce into a general conception of the Champagne community and its development.

The Commissioner is officially in charge. He possesses specific powers, signs decisions, presides at meetings and represents the organisation officially in all circumstances, as well as playing the role of arbiter and conciliator. He, the President of the Merchants and the President of the Vine-growers are the main movers of the organisation.

Working with them is the Consultative Committee, or the decision-making part of the CIVC. Composed of equal numbers of vine-growers and merchants (including both presidents), it meets as often as necessary and deals with everything of interest to the two sides. No decision is taken without the unanimous agreement of its members.

Reporting to the Consultative Committee are ten specialist committees, which correspond to the various activities of the CIVC, including the technical, oenological, viticultural and legal aspects. To give an example, in 1986 various working groups were asked to prepare the basis for a Charter of Quality. Since then, the adoption of a Quality Charter has been recommended and covers soil analysis before planting and replanting, the use of a proper mix of clones, the definition of quality of the grapes on a sliding scale, and the agreement on pressing centres and standards required. Currently, all the press houses in the region are being examined and either eliminated or brought up to standard.

The CIVC is a powerful organisation which also organises any research programmes, assists with technical advice and produces the statistics. And among other things, it looks after the good name of Champagne throughout the world, taking legal action where necessary. If it does sometimes seem to do so unnecessarily and with a heavy hand, as perhaps in the Elderflower Champagne or Champagne Perry (Babycham) cases, it is worth remembering the earlier battles to establish the name and to combat fraudulent practices.

Undoubtedly the most significant case since the Second World War concerned 'Spanish Champagne', initially lost but then won in the English courts. It arose from the discovery that an enterprise named the Costa Brava Wine Company was selling a Spanish sparkling wine called Perelada, not even produced by the traditional method but labelled as Spanish Champagne. The venture was the brainchild of Michael Grylls and backed by Spanish money. The question concerned which way to proceed: whether to bring a criminal prosecution which would involve a large amount of publicity and a jury trial, or whether to bring a civil action for 'passing off' a product as something it clearly was not.

Initially, the CIVC opted for criminal proceedings, which involved proving that it was deliberately misleading to label Perelada as champagne, even with the qualifying word 'Spanish'. This turned out to be a mistake. Public sympathy was on the side of the young man and his company, and the publicity rebounded when, at Christmas 1958, the jury found for the defendant. The Champenois were not to be deterred and came back for a second round, this time in the civil courts. In *Bollinger and others* v. *Costa Brava Wine Company*, the Champenois had to prove not only that to name the wine champagne was false and misleading, but also that it was damaging to the reputation of champagne in that deceived purchasers believed it to be the authentic article. It was on this second point, difficult to argue and prove, that in the end the whole case turned.

Counsel for the Champenois was Geoffrey Lawrence, QC. The defence lawyers had found plenty of similar cases. Since Britain was not then a signatory to the Treaty of Rome, French *appellation* law had no bearing at that time; there was Australian 'Burgundy', Spanish 'Sauternes', white 'Chianti', Spanish 'Chablis', Cyprus 'Sherry' and many more. Meanwhile, on the hubristic assumption that they would win again, the defendants produced a booklet entitled *Giving a Champagne Party*.

The defence was represented by Sir Milner Holland, QC. He called only a handful of witnesses, all of whom were happy to point out that the term 'Spanish' clearly showed that the wine did not originate in the Champagne region of France. According to André Simon, one witness stated that to call Perelada 'champagne' was far more attractive than calling it sparkling wine. The weight of the evidence, however, showed that the term 'champagne' had never been used generically until the arrival of Perelada. André Simon himself was a witness and when asked about Spanish 'chablis' replied that the growers in Chablis had been too poor to fight a similar case.

On the afternoon of 6 December the matter came to a head. The judge posed a hypothetical question. If some ignorant person orders champagne, but says to the waiter that it seems expensive and is then offered Perelada as an alternative, would the waiter not add, 'But of course that is not French champagne'? Mr Lawrence grabbed his chance. 'My Lord, if he said, "Not French champagne", he would mean "It is not French champagne it is Spanish champagne, but whether you have French champagne or Spanish champagne it is still champagne." ' This, in essence, was the case. On 16 December Mr Justice Danckwerts pronounced judgment for the champagne houses. Perelada could no longer style itself champagne, and all such labels had to be changed within forty-eight hours. Interestingly enough, the Costa Brava Wine Company changed its directors at the same time.

It was a major legal triumph. Henceforth within the United Kingdom, the Commonwealth and any dependencies, champagne could only come from the small area in north-eastern France dignified by that name.

At approximately the same time, a new method of pricing the grapes at harvest was developing. Until the end of the 1930s, there had been no compulsion on the merchant houses to buy the grapes, and, as discussed previously, if the quality was poor, or even if it was good but stocks in the cellars were too high, many houses would not or could not purchase. One of the driving factors behind the CIVC was to ensure that the growers could make a living.

In 1959, 'the Contract' was first signed by those growers who had grapes to sell, guaranteeing what proportion of their harvest would go into the system. In essence, the CIVC acted as a clearing house for these grapes, funnelling them through to the buying houses. In practice, of course, the major houses were always able to obtain grapes from those areas which traditionally made part of their blends. Each house, however, was restricted to a total purchasing quantity tied to the previous year's production to ensure that smaller houses could also purchase sufficient grapes for their requirements. This contract was renewable every six years, and it was the refusal of the growers to commit sufficient grapes at the end of the 1980s that caused a change of system which, in part, led to the enormous price rises of 1990.

The price set for the grapes was derived via a mathematical formula. It was known that the cost of the grapes was about 34 per cent of the final price of a bottle when it left the cellar door. Since every producer had to submit a return giving details of bottles sold and their price, from basic inexpensive wines to the great *cuvées de prestige* such as Dom Pérignon, Krug Grande Cuvée and Roederer Cristal, the calculation was simple. Divide the number of bottles sold into the total price received and the result is the cost of an 'average' bottle of champagne. Take 34 per cent of that and this figure gives the price of 1 kilo of grapes. For the purpose of this exercise, which is now consigned to history, 1 kilo was taken as the amount needed to create one bottle of champagne.

After this figure had been arrived at, a 10 per cent tolerance either way was permitted. This was based on the state of the market, rising or falling demand, conditions of the vintage about to take place and stocks in the cellars. About fourteen days before the harvest the figure, agreed between the President of the growers and the President of the makers, with the Commissioner acting as referee if necessary, was published. This price applied to grapes from the *grand cru* sites (100 per cent). Lower down the *échelle*, the price was proportionate.

There are a very large number of people who work, one way or another, in the champagne industry. These include the bottle manufacturers, the cork makers, those who make the capsules and wine muzzles, print the labels and provide the foil. But the main source of employment is, of course, the product itself. The trade is divided into three main sectors: the houses, the growers and the co-operatives.

The 120 houses vary tremendously in size. About 50 per cent of the trade goes through the top ten houses, while at the bottom are a number of tiny houses, little more than growers. The houses initially took the place of the monasteries, buying from the growers and making the wine. They are known as *négociants manipul-ants*, and the initials NM appear with the matriculation number on the label. Many of these houses have some vineyards of their own and rely on bought-in grapes to supplement their own, although a number, including Alfred Gratien, have none.

The growers, or *récoltants*, own the vastly greater part of the vineyard area, and even today most sell their grapes to the houses or co-operatives. Some 5,000, however, make and market wine under their own label, a move which began in 1934 and gained very considerable momentum during the late 1950s and 1960s. Most of their wine is sold from the premises, often to regular customers who bring their cars and return time and again. Every village in Champagne has its local growers signposted at the cross-roads and advertising on walls and doors.

Excellent though some of these wines can be, it has to be admitted that if champagne is truly a blended wine, the *récoltant* can be at a disadvantage. Although some own plots in different villages, very often the holding is in one piece and because of situation they may well grow only one variety, thus very much restricting the style that can be made. If one remains a *récoltant manipulant*, the crop can only be enlarged by purchasing a maximum of 5 per cent over and above their own grapes, so the scope for balancing and blending the wine in poorer years is very slight. It is always open to such growers to change and apply for registration as *négociants manipulants*, and some very successful ones have done so, but the ability to purchase grapes has to be set against the financial implications of buying them and the loss of tax advantages.

Just as the post-war period saw a significant growth in *récoltants manipulants*, so too there was a strong expansion of the co-operative movement which had begun in 1934. This move was strongly supported by the CIVC. Not all co-operatives exist to make the complete wine. Some purely exist to press grapes, while others press and vinify the still wines. A third type takes the process as far as inducing the second fermentation, but does not finish the wine by putting it through ageing, *remuage* and *dégorgement*, while the *coopérative manipulante* completes the entire method and sells the wine under its own label or labels, and may also return completed bottles to some of its members who then sell under their labels. The matriculation number on a co-operative label will be preceded by the initials CM.

In addition to these three major areas of the champagne trade, there is another way in which the wines are marketed and sold. Some firms act purely as wholesalers, buying the finished wine and selling it on, usually under an own-brand name. They are called *négociants non-manipulants*. Sometimes, though not invariably, these businesses act as brokers for Buyer's Own Brand (BOB) champagnes. These wines are known by the name of the retail outlet or restaurant, or other outlet, and frequently come from major sources, such as Duval Leroy, or large co-operatives like the Centre Viticole de la Champagne in Chouilly, but may also be supplied by a wholesaling *négociant*. BOBs appear also with many fine-wine firms, as well as with supermarkets such as Tesco, Waitrose or Sainsbury. So Averys of Bristol, Tanners of Shrewsbury, Berry Bros. & Rudd and Lay & Wheeler, for example, list champagnes under their own label.

Wines in this sector of the market carry the initials MA before the number. This represents *marque d'acheteur* when it appears on a Buyer's Own Brand label, but may also stand for *marque auxiliaire*, meaning a *sous-marque* or secondary brand name.

13

Les Champenois

The total legally defined area for the production of champagne is 34,500 hectares, virtually unaltered from the final decision on the vineyards set out in 1919. The physical area that may be planted is smaller at 31,050 hectares, taking into account thoroughfares and buildings. This is a very small production region for a wine in such demand. And because of the need to replace the vines at regular intervals leaving some ground as non-productive for a few years, as no grapes may be harvested for AOC wine until the vine is at least three years old, it has been calculated that there can never be more than 29,000 hectares in actual production at any given time.

Of this area, only about 14 per cent is owned by producing houses. Some, indeed, have no vineyards at all and rely completely on purchasing all required grapes, while others have vineyards of their own supplying anything between 15 to 95 per cent of their needs. Thus it is clear that vineyard ownership is critical to the functioning of la Champagne Viticole. By the early 1980s there were just over 14,000 growers. Today that number has increased to about 16,000. (It is sometimes quoted at 18,500, but the lower figure is more likely to be accurate.) Few of these growers own more than 5 hectares, and by far the largest number have less than 1, and 1 hectare is believed to be the absolute minimum at which it is possible to make some sort of living out of wine production.

As has been shown, right throughout its history, Champagne has always relied on a particular and unique system. Under the *ancien régime*, the peasants grew the grapes which were made into wine, usually by the monks. The establishment of a sparkling wine led to the development of merchant houses, the early ones often having dealt in woollen and other materials then changed direction. Come the Revolution of 1789 and the dispossession of the monasteries, the making of the wine passed almost totally into the hands of these winemakers, and the nineteenth century saw the rise of the majority of those known today. Inevitably this put the commercial power firmly in the hands of the merchants, or *négociants*. The weak link in the chain, however, remained the numerous growers; so long as they were prepared to sell their grapes, the whole system worked. But in the years since the Second World War, and particularly as demand on the French market soared, a larger number of these *récoltants* began to make their own wines. Sometimes the production was just sufficient for personal use, but more often it was designed for sale.

Out of the *récoltants* who work their own holdings on a full-time basis (for some are only part-time), a substantial number are now producing and selling wine under their own label as *récoltants manipulants* and their production has become significant. This development started during the 1950s, as the old suspicions that the merchant houses were extremely wealthy at the growers' expense resurfaced. It began slowly, because it was a financially risky decision. The cost of purchasing the necessary equipment was high, and the method itself dictated that it would be longer than usual before any wine could be sold. Production rose from a million or so bottles to today's figure of 63 million and much of this was during the 1970s when the domestic French market discovered these wines. Additionally, as tourism flourished, the visitor with a car began to enjoy finding a small grower whose wines could be purchased at a good price. Many returned on a regular basis, often having become not only a customer but now a friend.

Not all growers market any or all of their grapes as wine. Many sell either to the *négociant* houses or to the co-operatives. In the latter case, sometimes the wines made by co-operatives are in fact sold under a *récoltant* label by members of that co-operative, in which case it is not a true grower's wine.

The enormous rise in the demand for champagne during the 1980s put a strain on the supply of grapes, with an ever-growing demand for wine in all sections of the trade – *négociants*, *récoltants* and co-operatives alike. The demand seemed never-ending. Virtually all possible vineyard areas were now planted. Overproduction from the vines and a haste to satisfy the market saw a large number of wines rushed through the process as fast as the law allowed, and sent out while still green but with this youth and thinness compensated for by heavy *dosage*. Indeed, such was the production frenzy that when the market collapsed in the early 1990s, it was rumoured that there were in the region of 12 million speculative bottles lying *sur lattes*, made in expectation of the market continuing to grow.

The Contract for the regulation of the supply of grapes and their prices had worked well and all parties seemed satisfied with it. However, when it was up for renewal in 1989, at the very height of demand, everyone knew that it was now at risk. Many growers subscribing to the Contract were openly criticising the large houses who had let the bottle prices rise quite considerably during the boom period. The growers felt that they were not benefiting from increased demand. The houses responded by pointing out that unless rationing by price was introduced they would be forced to limit supplies to their customers, which might well be illegal under the Treaty of Rome. Equally, many small *négociant* houses suspected that the big houses were using this as an excuse to squeeze some of them out, since few small houses could achieve such a high rate of profitability.

As it happened, the growers settled the question. For the very first time, assuming of course that the market would continue to grow, they felt strongly that the commercial strength was with them. Of the vineyards which produced the all-important raw material for the product in demand, champagne, 85.7 per cent belonged to them. The inevitable happened. The amount of grapes which they were prepared to commit to the houses through the Contract was too small for the system to work. It had failed, and a completely new situation arose.

The CIVC declared a 'free' market would exist on a trial basis for the next three years. For the first time the houses could buy grapes not through the Contract, but directly from the growers. But in some respects it was certainly not 'free'. Every sale had to be logged with the CIVC to ensure there would be sufficient grapes to go round and that smaller houses were not pushed out by the financial clout of the big ones. Secondly, the CIVC would set a reference price for the grapes, and no one would have to pay more. This price, as in the Contract, would apply to grapes from the 100 per cent villages.

That was the theory; in practice, things were very different. In advance of the harvest, houses large and small were concerned about the actual price they would have to pay. The guideline price was set at Ff32.50, as compared with about Ff25 the previous year. As it is recognised that 34 per cent of the cost of a bottle of champagne at the cellar door is the cost of the grapes, this was a large extra cost. However, the market now being free, this price could not in fact be enforced, and some houses admitted privately that they had been compelled to pay considerably more to obtain grapes of their desired quality.

This was to have an immediate effect on the prices. Although the grapes being bought and vinified at this increased cost would not be released for some years, prices began to rise immediately and very steeply in all sectors of the market. The inexpensive supermarket brands at, say, £8.99 suddenly cost £9.99 and went on rising during the autumn and Christmas period of 1990. Top-quality wines also rocketed, and middle-range bottles did the same. This provoked an enormous consumer reaction led by the wine press. Everyone asked why the increases came so long before the wines affected by this price rise: a perfectly fair question.

The answer lies mainly in the way the stocks are financed. Because of the delay in being able to recoup the capital outlay of buying the grapes, it is customary for the stocks lying in the cellars to be financed by borrowed money on which interest has to be paid. So a far greater price for the grapes often meant heavier borrowing commitments to be met instantly. Therefore, some increase in the price of wines just appearing on the market was absolutely inevitable.

The Champenois, however, have always been happy to shroud their workings in mystery, and failed to see any need to explain themselves to their customers. This hubris brought its own reward. Articles appeared with titles such as 'Is this the end for Champagne?' and 'Has the bubble burst?' Respected and influential wine writers encouraged their readers to look elsewhere for bottles of bubbly, and the general public, appalled by what they perceived as sheer greed, voted with their purses. The bubble of the 1980s had indeed burst and Champagne was plunged into a deep economic crisis. Although two-thirds of production is sold on the domestic market, a tremendous amount of this is from growers and co-operatives. Conversely, the export market, apart from the Buyer's Own Brand sector, tended to comprise the prestigious names and, although totalling only one-third of sales, is very important in financial terms. The export market collapsed; it was some 55 per cent down.

To be absolutely fair, the enormous price increases were not the entire reason for this disaster. In the euphoria of the late 1980s, only a very few far-sighted makers realised that a recession depression was almost upon the major industrial economies and would depress sales, whatever the price, and those few did try to stem the rush for grapes that had such catastrophic results on prices paid. The Gulf War, too, would have had something of the same effect. Inside Champagne, both growers and makers were appalled. Sales had collapsed, and the growers were only too aware that the houses blamed them for the situation, believing that it was the unreasonable (to them) greed of the growers that had led to this catastrophe, while the growers, seeing the unsold stocks in the cellars growing, began to fear that there might not be a market for their grapes in the 1991 harvest. Indeed, with that harvest, prices began to settle back.

Recriminations aside, much good was to come out of the crisis. After the over-production of the 1980s, improvement of quality became the watchword. Production levels per hectare were lowered. The reduction in the amount of juice at pressing virtually eliminated the *deuxième taille* – an initiative previously discussed but conveniently forgotten in boom times. The minimum length of time on the lees was extended to fifteen months, it being felt that a desired eighteen months was unobtainable all at once. All systems throughout the method were examined. The CIVC issued a Quality Charter for press-houses and began inspections. The *négociant* houses, now able to purchase grapes directly, began to work with their chosen growers to help improve the quality.

From the consumers' point of view, the news was also good. Prices dropped back – but to a degree, it has to be said, that is still causing serious financial problems within Champagne – and quality at all levels began to improve owing to the simple reason that stocks in the cellars, growing as wines remained unsold, were receiving considerable extra ageing. Indeed, the (barely) two and a half years' stock found at the end of the 1980s rose steadily to four years' worth or more.

In the end, it may be that everyone will have benefited. Sales began to improve on export markets at the end of 1991, although the domestic market went into recession and has been slow to recover. The problem remains one of price, with a number of houses changing hands or being bought for the first time, and there is no doubt that many are struggling financially. To try to stabilise the market, growers and makers have agreed to a set price for grapes contractually, with at most a 3 per cent tolerance, for the next five years. Whether this will be sufficient, only the future will tell.

14

The Grandes Marques

This title is rather ambiguous, simply meaning a famous (or great) brands. In the popular imagination, however, it has come to suggest something very special – so much so, in fact, that houses which are not members of the syndicate but recognised as producing very good wines have frequently been referred to as Grandes Marques.

Although the Syndicat des Grandes Marques de Champagne came into being under that name only in 1964, its history is much longer. It began life in 1882 as the Syndicat du Commerce des Vins de Champagne, a trade association made up of the major merchant houses of the time, with the declared intention of defending the professional interests of its members. The original statutes have since been amended six times, and then again, as a draft, finally on 2 September 1993.

From the beginning the syndicate had considerable influence. Although not fully appreciated by the small growers, many members did help a great deal in combating the phylloxera blight and in replanting with the new grafted vines; and from the very beginning they fought hard to open up export markets and to promote free trade. Among their other objectives was the determination to seek improvement in quality at all times, and to defend, through the courts if necessary, the name and the region of la Champagne Viticole.

In 1964 the syndicate changed its form, and became the Syndicat des Grandes Marques known today. Its membership included (in alphabetical order) Ayala, Billecart-Salmon, Bollinger, Veuve Clicquot-Ponsardin, Delbeck, Deutz, Heidsieck Monopole, Charles Heidsieck, Irroy, Krug, Lanson, Masse, Moët & Chandon, Montebello, Mumm, Perrier-Jouët, Joseph Perrier, Piper-Heidsieck, Pol Roger, Pommery, Ch. & A. Prieur, Louis Roederer, Ruinart, Salon and Taittinger. Since that date four more houses have been elected as members: Laurent-Perrier, Mercier, Henriot and Canard-Duchêne, but a number of the original houses have either disappeared or become the *sous-marques* of other merchants.

On 2 September 1993, an Extraordinary General Meeting took place, called by Jean-Claude Rouzaud of Louis Roederer, President of the syndicate, to take stock of the situation, for all of Champagne was in crisis. The collapse of the market following the boom in demand during the 1980s had created very serious problems indeed. In addition, it was quite openly commented upon that the syndicate, which after all claimed to lead on quality, contained members who did not deserve such status, while other houses with a better claim to quality were being denied entry. This EGM produced a new strategy.

The press release of a few weeks later, dated 21 October, makes it very clear. Having stated the historic position and aims of the Syndicat, it went on to state that the 28 houses had approved a change in their statutes.

> The distinctive quality of Grande Marque Champagnes and their methods of international distribution will henceforth be governed by a definite pact. With the idea that stringent regulations and will-power alone can secure their own interests and serve in the best possible way the future interests of the entire Champagne-growing area, the Grandes Marques have created for themselves requirements which are even more scrupulous than the rules of the *appellation*, and intend to increase the recognition of the brands and the Champagne region, the world over. The reason for this approach is simple. A price war has understandably broken out owing to the crisis which has hit demand. After the turmoil of 1991, Champagne began to regain lost ground, but this recovery came through low-priced Champagnes creating a risk that the nature of Champagne supply would be permanently modified, bringing with it an upheaval of the foundations of the Champagne economy.

Reading this, one must also remember that one house, Bollinger, had already issued a stringent Quality Charter by which it was operating (see p. 158).

This EGM also announced that there would be an audit of all members against this strengthened set of draft regulations, designed to make sure that all the Grande Marque houses were operating to the same quality criteria. These were considerably higher than those demanded by the AOC laws, and in essence very similar to what the Charta Association in the Rheingau had instigated in the early 1980s. Moreover, this audit for the very first time was also to cover commercial policy, with a particular view to ensuring that prices charged were commensurate with intrinsic quality, since it was felt very strongly that any member with an aggressive pricing policy would inevitably be cutting corners, which in turn would certainly compromise standards.

No sooner was this audit announced than rumours were rife about which house, or houses, would fail. The initial idea had been that any member who regarded the new regulations as too stringent could simply resign quietly, without any public scandal, and that those whose results were uncertain could be given the option of a trial period, probably of about three years, in which to try to meet the new criteria. But in the event, all this was for nothing. Finally M. Rouzaud, who had spent three years negotiating the new deal, could not gain total agreement on the new quality parameters. These included sourcing of the grapes, and the ban on buying wine *sur lattes*,* use of first-pressing musts only, an agreed minimum time on the lees considerably longer than that stipulated by the *appellation* laws, and an agreement to charge prices that would give a fair return on costs.

Rather than continue the arguments, which had now run from 1993 until 1996, it was felt that since no agreement could be reached between the members on the draft higher minimum standards, it would be better to disband the syndicate. This finally happened in the summer of 1997. Since then, protection of the interests of the houses concerned has reverted to the Union des Maisons de Champagne.

Although the Syndicat des Grandes Marques was at best a semi-

---

* Mention needs to be made of the '*sur lattes* scandal'. Although many Champenois believe that this was blown out of proportion, the fact remains that for any house finding itself short of saleable stock to buy in bottles from another source lying *sur lattes*, to add their own *dosage* and then sell on under its own label, is, to put it mildly, hoodwinking the customer. Although a long-established custom and not actually illegal, it is a practice that does nothing for the image of the region. Interestingly enough, the endeavour to outlaw the practice, proposed during the audit of the Grande Marque houses, was apparently one of the reasons which led to the disbandment of the group.

official body, in principle it did represent the public face of excellence in Champagne. Its disbandment means that there is now no body of producers acting in concert in the interests of the highest quality and this leaves a serious gap. It is highly unlikely that the efforts of individual houses per se, such as Roederer, Bollinger or Krug, can influence the public view of Champagne in the way that the Syndicat des Grandes Marques undoubtedly did, and it does seem very sad that 115 years of history have been abandoned.

At present it appears that each of the former Grandes Marques has decided to put all its efforts into improving the quality and worldwide standing of its own brand. But perhaps the best answer would be for another 'syndicate' to come into being, no doubt made up of a smaller number of probably different houses determined to fly the flag of the finest quality.

15
The Makers

There are many houses, both large and small, making and selling wine in Champagne, not to mention the hundreds if not thousands of *récoltants manipulants* and co-operatives, and any choice between them is rather invidious. Nonetheless not all can be included, and the profiles which follow have been selected from not necessarily the biggest or most important, but from interesting businesses of all three types. They are listed alphabetically.

HENRI ABELÉ

Originally founded in 1757 by Théodore Vander Veken, this house is the third oldest still trading. In 1834 Théodore's great-nephew, Auguste Ruinart de Brimont, took as his partner none other than Antoine Müller, who had assisted the Veuve Clicquot in developing the *pupitres* for *remuage*. From this partnership the house passed into the control of the Abelé de Müller family, and it is worth noting that it was in their cellars in 1884 that Armand Walfart developed *dégorgement à la glace*. In 1903 the name of the house was changed to Abelé-Vander Veken. In 1942 control passed to the Compagnie Française des Grands Vins (by an ironic twist, founded by Eugène Charmat, who in 1909 had invented the bulk method of making sparkling wine, *cuve close*) and then in 1985 it was bought by the giant Cava firm, Freixenet. Apparently the head of the Spanish company, José Ferrer Sala, so appreciated a bottle he had tried that he decided to buy the company! The wines tend to be on the very dry side, owing to a high Chardonnay content in most of the *cuvées*. The NV is named Sourire de Reims after the famous angel, the *rosé* is made by skin contact and not by blending, the vintage is named Grande Marque Impérial, while in only the very best years the house makes a prestige *cuvée*, Blanc de Blancs Réserve du Repas.

52 rue de Sillery, 51051 Reims, tel.: 26 87 79 80

AYALA

This house owes its name to Edmond d'Ayala, the son of a Colombian diplomat who married Gabrielle d'Albrecht, part of whose dowry was a vineyard in Mareuil. He founded the house in 1860 and, owing to a close friendship with the Gilbey family, the wines swiftly became known in Britain. Now owned by Jean-Michel Ducellier, who has also acquired Château La Lagune in the Haut-Médoc, it is still an independent house with a reputation for quality, most particularly for its vintage wines. Styles of wine made are Brut NV, Brut Vintage, Rosé and Demi-Sec, but more recently they have developed a vintage Blanc de Blancs made from 100 per cent *échelle*-rated grapes only, which is both creamy and elegant, outstanding of its type.

Ayala also own the house established in 1834 by the Duc de Montebello. The house now makes a Brut NV and vintage wines, both based heavily on Pinot Noir, but with Pinot Meunier and Chardonnay in the blends. Also produced are NV Sec and Demi-Sec.

Château d'Aÿ, 2 boulevard du Nord, 51160 Aÿ-Champagne, tel.: 26 55 15 44

BARANCOURT

In 1966 Jean-Paul Brice, Pierre Martin and Raynald Tritant pooled their resources to purchase some extra vineyards. In 1969 they joined the family holdings with the newly planted vineyards to form a new house named after a prestigious champagne house of Bouzy, which had fallen into disuse. All three young men were graduates – Tritant in accountancy, the other two in viticulture. Since then the house has developed a high reputation for *vins de garde*, rather hard in their youth but ageing extremely well. The styles produced are Brut Réserve NV, Blanc de Blancs, Rosé Grand Cru, a *monocru* Bouzy Brut which spends a long time in the cellars before release, usually a vintage, and a very interesting Coteaux Champenois vintage Bouzy Rouge from 100 per cent Pinot Noir.

These are wines for long ageing. In 1994, the house was sold to Vranken-Lafitte (see page 136).

Place André Tritant, 51150 Bouzy, tel.: 26 57 00 67

BEAUMONT DES CRAYÈRES

Founded in 1955, this is a champagne co-operative with a high reputation for quality and value. In part this may be due to the fact that the average holding of the members is only half a hectare, which allows for very careful control of the grapes. Certainly in recent years the wines have been highly praised in markets as distant as America, as well as in France and Britain. A high proportion of the grapes used are Pinot Meunier, at least 50 per cent in their NV Brut Réserve, and also in their Rosé, which has excellent fruit. Two other wines are their Cuvée de Prestige, normally about equal parts of all three grape varieties, and the very special vintage Cuvée Spéciale Nostalgie made from Chardonnay alone.

64 rue de la Liberté, Mardeuil, 51200 Epernay, tel.: 26 55 29 40

BILLECART-SALMON

This house has had a somewhat chequered history since it was founded in 1818 by Nicolas-François when he entered the champagne trade. An early reputation for quality opened up overseas markets, but in 1830 a massive loss caused by a thoroughly incompetent agent in New York checked its advance, and it was not until 1917 that matters improved. Charles-Roland Billecart rebuilt the business, and sold the vineyards to finance further expansion, a decision which has proved sound, with steady growth in the business. The house has acquired 10 ha. of vineyard and it has a well-deserved reputation for very high quality wines, seemingly delicate and with great finesse, which is rather misleading since they are capable of great ageing. Modern handling of the must avoids all oxidation. The house styles include a Brut NV with a high proportion (one-third) of Pinot Meunier, as well as slightly sweeter wines, a Sec and a Demi-Sec, a very fine vintage Blanc de Blancs with a superb mousse and a long, delicate finish, a good Rosé made by blending in 8 per cent red Pinot Noir from their own vineyards, and the vintage Cuvée Nicolas-François named after the firm's founder.

40 rue Carnot, 51530 Mareuil-sur-Aÿ, tel.: 26 52 60 22

H. BLIN & CO.

Blin is the name of a co-operative established in the Marne Valley in 1947. Most of the members' vineyards grow Pinot Meunier grapes, so the styles tend to be round and fruity. Production at present includes a Blanc de Noirs, Brut Tradition, an easy-drinking, attractive wine, Brut Réserve, made of their best *cuvées* of black grapes together with some 20 per cent Chardonnay, offering a more complex and elegant style, a Rosé, and a vintage wine made in only the very best years. These wines represent good value.

5 rue de Verdun, BP 35, 51700 Vincelles, tel.: 26 58 20 04

BOIZEL

A small house begun in 1834 by Auguste and Julie Boizel, its current head is Auguste's great-great-granddaughter, Evelyne Roques-Boizel, who became head of the house in 1984. Heavy investments have been made in stainless steel, new premises, temperature control and a new quality-control laboratory. In the last ten years production has almost doubled but without any loss of quality. Five *cuvées* are offered these days, a Brut Rosé, very highly regarded and made from all three grapes, the classic Brut Réserve, with good fruity taste, a Brut Blanc de Blancs, made with grapes from the Côte des Blancs only, which was relaunched to celebrate the 150th anniversary of the firm in 1984, a Grand Vintage, and finally the *cuvée de prestige*, Joyau de France, a powerful style dominated by Pinot Noir.

16 rue de Bernon, 51205 Epernay, tel.: 26 55 21 51

J. BOLLINGER

This is one of the undoubted great names of Champagne, founded in 1829 by Jacques Bollinger, originally from Württemberg, and Paul Renaudin, a Champenois who remained with the firm only for a short while although his name stayed on the label for many years. M. Bollinger married a daughter of the Comte de Villermont by a second marriage and started to enlarge the vineyard holdings. This policy, which was continued by his sons, has stood the company is very good stead, since today the vineyards provide about 70 per cent of the company's needs. The company has shipped supplies to Britain since 1865, and was said to be a great favourite of the Prince of Wales, Edward VII-to-be. The grandson of the original founder, another Jacques, took over the company in 1918 and he too extended the vineyards, but, too ill to fight during the Second World War, he died in 1941 and control passed to his widow, the redoubtable Mme Lily Bollinger who again enlarged the vineyards. Seen bicycling around the estate, Mme Lily was fanatical about quality, but still managed to double the production during her lifetime without sacrificing standards. When she died in 1977, control passed to her nephew, Christian Bizot, and today the company is headed by Ghislain de Montgolfier, her great-nephew. In 1990, faced with the mounting criticism of the quality of many champagnes in view of the huge price rises, Bollinger produced their Charter of Ethics and Quality, to which they do adhere.

The vast majority of their vineyards are classified as *grand cru*, with 30 per cent *premier cru*, and only a few others outside that level. Quality of grapes is all-important to them. First-pressing juice only is used and a percentage is vinified in oak. Time on the lees is long, to give the wines the Bollinger style. The Special Cuvée, the NV, is full, rich and dry. The vintage styles include Grande Année and a Rosé from the best years. The house is famous for its RD or Recently Disgorged wine, which is the Grande Année with many extra years on the lees. This can sometimes appear too aged for some palates, but is complex wine that needs to accompany food. The Vieilles Vignes Françaises, made from the two tiny parcels of Pinot Noir which escaped phylloxera, is a curiosity. Undoubtedly a rich, well-aged, long wine, nevertheless it can sometimes appear clumsy when compared with a blend.

16 rue Jules-Lobet, 51160 Aÿ-Champagne, tel.: 26 53 33 66

ALEXANDRE BONNET

A leading producer in the Aube, its Pinot Noir vineyards cover just over 35 hectares round Les Riceys, supplying most of its needs, although Chardonnay is purchased in the Côte des Blancs. Serge and Alain Bonnet make the blends, and produce an NV Cuvée Tradition, which is a very drinkable, and a fruity Blanc de Noirs, as well as a Cuvée Prestige, a Blanc de Blancs and a Brut Rosé. Very competent champagnes indeed, but one of the specialities is the rare Rosé des Riceys, where 20 per cent of the grapes are still trodden, and a rich, smoky red Coteaux Champenois.

138 rue du Général de Gaulle, 10340 Les Riceys, tel.: 25 29 30 93

CANARD-DUCHÊNE

Founded in 1868 by a M. Canard who had married a Mlle Duchêne, its early history is uncertain as the house's records were destroyed during the First World War, but its real period of growth came during the 1950s. In 1973 Piper-Heidsieck obtained a one-third share of the company, but in 1978 sold this to Veuve Clicquot who then became the owners. Consequently, the house is now part of the LVMH group.

This house is known for the variable quality of its wines, notably the NV, in spite of a well-equipped, modern winery. However, the vintage wines are of an excellent standard.

1 rue Edmond Canard, Ludes, 51500 Rilly-la-Montagne, tel.: 26 61 10 96

CATTIER

The house of Cattier is a family business dating back to at least 1763, although the champagne firm was founded only in 1920. The wholly owned vineyards supply almost all the grapes required, and are all *premier cru* on the *échelle*. They make Brut NV, Vintage and Brut Rosé, all of which spend plenty of time on the lees and are well aged. Their top wine, however, is a *monocru*, the Clos du Moulin, 2.2 hectares in size. It was acquired in 1950 and the first wine made in 1952. Made from an equal percentage of Pinot Noir and Chardonnay, it is a remarkable wine with both finesse, elegance and the ability to age. It has just been chosen for the British Airways Concorde flights.

6/11 rue Dom Pérignon, 51500 Chigny-les-Roses, tel.: 26 03 42 11

DEUTZ & GELDERMANN

Founded in 1838 by two immigrants from Aachen (Aix-la-Chapelle), William Deutz, who was a *négociant*, and Pierre Geldermann, a champagne salesman, this is a high-quality but often underrated house. Initially without vineyards, today the family owns vineyards which satisfy 40 per cent of production needs, and between them rate at least 97 on the *échelle*. Free-run *cuvée* juice only is used, and no fining or filtration takes place. The wines are left on the lees for some time, are disgorged by hand and are given an additional six months in bottle in the cellars before release for sale. The present head of the house is André Lallier-Deutz who also owns Delas Frères in the Rhône, but since 1993 the controlling interest has been bought by Louis Roederer. All styles are made, including a very fine Blanc de Blancs with an elegant mousse, and the top wine is Cuvée William Deutz which is made only in the very best years. Rich, long, full of flavour and balance, it is a magnificent bottle.

16 rue Jeanson, 51160 Aÿ-Champagne, tel.: 26 55 15 11

CHAMPAGNE VEUVE A. DEVAUX

This is a co-operative label produced by the Union Auboise, a powerful grouping of growers controlling about 1,300 hectares planted mainly with Pinot Noir, a tiny percentage of Meunier and about 12 per cent Chardonnay. The wines are gaining market share fairly rapidly; in blind tastings they come out very well, and they are excellent value for money. One reason for this is that there is no haste in producing these wines and they are all properly aged before release. The Grande Réserve Brut NV could almost be described as a textbook champagne, and they have recently made and are about to release a very interesting Blanc de Noirs. Additionally they make a vintage wine in good years, as well as a Rosé and some Rosé des Riceys.

Domaine de Villeneuve, 10110 Bar-sur-Seine, tel.: 25 29 85 57

ANDRÉ DRAPPIER

The Drappier family have been wine-growers in Urville in the Aube since Napoleonic times and boast twelfth-century cellars. More recently General de Gaulle, in retirement at his home near by, was a regular customer.

As might be expected from an Auboise house, the wines are heavily dominated by Pinot Noir and not only show technical expertise, but also have a strong personality of their own. Their Brut NV has a clean and generously fruity flavour. The vintage wines, which carry the date of disgorgement on the label, are always fine as is the *rosé*, Val des Demoiselles. The Prestige Cuvée of Grande Sendrée is highly stylish, particularly when allowed good bottle age.

Grand Rue, 10200 Urville, Bar-sur-Aube, tel.: 25 26 40 15

DUVAL LEROY

Situated at the bottom of the Côte des Blancs in Vertus, this family-owned house was founded in 1859, and most of its vineyards are either in the Côte des Blancs or Côte de Sézanne. Until recently most of its wines were sold under other labels, but since Carol Duval took over the running of the company following the death of her husband, there has been a move towards establishing the company name and reducing the amount of own-label wine, the current aim being a 50–50 split. Its non-vintage Fleur de Champagne is both delicate, elegant and flowery, well worth its name, and under the same name it produces a rich Blanc de Noirs, a Blanc de Blancs, Vintage, Rosé and Demi-Sec.

69 avenue de Bammental, 51130 Vertus, tel.: 26 52 10 75

ESTERLIN

Founded in 1948, and originally known as the Co-operative of Mancy, Esterlin at first only pressed the grapes but has been making champagne since 1953 and adopted its current name in 1984. It has 130 members with vineyards covering 120 hectares split between Sézanne, Mancy and a small amount on the Aisne. The name 'Esterlin' is of interest since, apparently, it is an old name for a currency in use during the Middle Ages. Apart from wine, Esterlin specialises in promoting the works of young and unknown artists which are on display, throughout the year, at their headquarters in Epernay.

At present, their range includes a Brut NV, a delicious Rosé with a long finish and an aroma of wild strawberries, a NV Blanc de Blancs, and a rich, powerful vintage wine, with a wonderful aroma of honey and dried fruit (at the time of writing it is the 1990 and made from 100 per cent Chardonnay). Finally, Esterlin have just produced a special wine for the Millennium, Cuvée Elzevia, again a *blanc de blancs* but sourced from *grand cru* sites only.

25 avenue de Champagne, 51200 Epernay, tel.: 26 59 71 52

NICOLAS FEUILLATTE

In the early 1970s, Nicolas Feuillatte, who had spent time working in New York and Sydney, inherited a 12-hectare vineyard, and began to create the champagne which bears his name. As a result of early success, it soon became obvious that he needed access to a far larger supply of grapes, and in 1986 he joined forces with the Centre Viticole de la Champagne, easily the largest and most modern winemaking plant in the region. The CVC based at Chouilly can call upon the production of at least 1,600 hectares, and this meant that the *crus* open to the Nicolas Feuillatte wines were excellent and very varied. The *marque* produces Réserve Particulière, a Brut NV, a Blanc de Blancs, a range of vintage wines from the best years and a Rosé. They are appealing wines with a fine creaming mousse and a rich flavour, although sometimes, for the British taste, a little more bottle age does improve them.

Chouilly, 51206 Epernay, tel.: 26 54 50 60

GEORGES GARDET

A highly traditional family firm whose vineyards are spread over 7 hectares in the *premier cru* villages of Chigny, Ludes and Rilly-la-Montagne. Additional grapes are bought from about thirty growers with whom the house has long-standing relationships. Their reserve wines are kept in oak. The house style is rich and well aged, mouth-filling and with an excellent mousse. Styles made are a range of *brut* NV (normally Brut Spécial is seen on the British market), Blanc de Blancs, Rosé, and vintage wines in the best years which are very well aged before release.

51500 Chigny-les-Roses, tel.: 26 03 42 03

GOSSET

In the Bibliothèque Nationale in Paris lies a document which clearly shows that a certain Pierre Gosset was not only a vine-grower but also a wine merchant at Aÿ in 1584. This establishes Gosset as the oldest house in Champagne still trading; in 1994, control passed to Frapin Cognac.

These wines attract those who love a rich, soft, well-aged style. Partially cask-fermented, the malolactic fermentation is avoided as the house believes this adds to both freshness and longevity. The Brut Excellence NV and the Grande Réserve NV both offer classic toasty aromas and weight of fruit, the latter being perhaps somewhat more elegant in style. Other styles include a Rosé, the Vintage Grand Millésime and the weighty, almost nutty Célébris.

69 rue Jules Blondeau, 51160 Aÿ-Champagne, tel.: 26 56 99 56

ALFRED GRATIEN

Established in Epernay in 1864, at the same time as their Loire house of Gratien & Meyer, this house makes distinguished and weighty wines with a nutty finish. An old-fashioned style, and no worse for that, these rich wines have a great appeal on the British market. No vineyards are owned. The first fermentation is in large oak casks, and the malolactic fermentation is blocked. The ageing is long – about four years for NV wines, which gain very considerable richness during this period. The basic NV Brut uses 67 per cent Pinot of both varieties, the remainder being Chardonnay, and has a wonderful bready aroma backed by the elegance and lightness of the white grapes. For vintage wines a higher proportion of Chardonnay tends to be used, and the house specialises in keeping old vintages which may be disgorged to order. The latest addition, Cuvée Paradis, is a most elegant wine, but does not carry a vintage date. It is delicious, with finesse, body and length.

30 rue Maurice Cerveaux, 51201 Epernay, tel.: 26 54 38 20

HEIDSIECK

Frequently confusion arises over the fact that three houses use the name Heidsieck. Florens-Louis Heidsieck came to Reims in 1777 originally to sell wool. In 1785 he started to sell wine but, as his son died young, three nephews came to help run the business, from whom are descended the three separate firms.

CHARLES HEIDSIECK

Charles-Camille Heidsieck, a great-nephew of Florens-Louis, went into partnership with Ernest Henriot in 1851, and shortly afterwards made the first of a number of journeys to the United States. There his wines became very popular, and his high-living lifestyle earned him the nickname 'Champagne Charlie', although his final visit ended as a suspected spy in a Unionist prison during the Civil War. Henriot left in 1875 and the firm stayed independent until bought in 1976, ironically enough by a descendant of Ernest Henriot, who subsequently sold it to Rémy-Cointreau, the Cognac-based group. The quality of the wines has improved markedly since then. With the financial support of the Rémy group, for the first time the firm has acquired vineyards of its own, all in top-quality areas, and the *chef des caves*, Daniel Thibault, has been able to purchase the best grapes. In addition, M. Thibault has built up his stocks of reserve wines. The Brut Réserve NV today represents a very fine style, creamy yet rich, slightly nutty on the finish, a remarkably complex wine. Their top wine, Blanc des Millénaires, always a vintage, is a magnificent *blanc de blancs* which frequently wins prizes and trophies.

Of particular interest on the marketing front, Charles Heidsieck are now putting the year in which the blend and second fermentation took place on the label to give the consumer some idea of the age of the wine. Three years are currently on offer: 1982, 1983 and 1984.

4 bld Henry Vasnier, 51055 Reims, tel.: 26 84 43 50

HEIDSIECK & CO. MONOPOLE

In 1834 Henri-Louis Walbaum, in partnership with his brother-in-law, commenced trading initially as Heidsieck & Co. The house remained in the family until 1923 when it came under the control of Edouard Mignon, who added Monopole to its title. In 1972 it passed to Seagram. It has big vineyard holdings in some very fine areas, but somehow in later days the quality has been somewhat ordinary. However, the prestige *cuvée*, Diamant Bleu, can be outstandingly good. The house has just been sold to Vranken-Lafitte (see page 136), and it will be interesting to see what the new owners do with it.

17 avenue de Champagne, 51205 Epernay, tel.: 26 59 50 50

PIPER-HEIDSIECK

Founded in 1835 by yet another nephew of Florens-Louis, Christian, who then died in the following year, the Piper name was added when his widow married Henri-Guillaume Piper two years later. The wines were always very popular in the United States. The firm's star salesman, Jean-Claude Kunkelmann, became a partner in the 1870s and Piper's heir. It remained a family business, passing through his daughter who was married to the Marquis d'Aulan, the war hero, but in 1989 it was taken over by the Rémy-Cointreau group. Since then, the wines have become rounder and richer, showing good fruit and, like those of Charles Heidsieck, are made by Daniel Thibault. In addition to the Brut NV and Brut Rosé, the firm introduced a vintage Brut Sauvage, completely undosed. At first this seemed an over-austere champagne, released a little early, but after a few extra years in bottle its true flavour and quality shone through. Their top wine, Champagne Rare, is delightful, light, zippy and full of delicate fruit.

51 boulevard Henri Vasnier, 51055 Reims, tel.: 26 84 43 00

HENRIOT

Wine-growers since the seventeenth century, in 1808 the house of Veuve Henriot Aîné began to make and sell champagne. In 1875, Ernest Henriot left Charles Heidsieck to take control of Veuve Henriot, the name of which was then changed to Henriot & Cie. He also acquired some prime vineyard sites on the Côte des Blancs. From 1976 until 1985 Henriot turned the clock back by taking control of Charles Heidsieck, then De Venoge and Troulliard. All three concerns were subsequently sold and for a short period Joseph Henriot, the current head, merged his house with Veuve Clicquot. More recently he has extended his interests outside Champagne to the Burgundy firm of Bouchard Père et Fils.

The style of the NV wines tends to be light and citrussy, but the vintage wines show very rich fruit although remaining dry on the finish.

3 place des Droits de l'Homme, 51100 Reims, tel.: 26 89 53 00.

JACQUESSON & FILS

Founded at the end of the 1789 Revolution by Claude Jacquesson and his son Memmie, this was a favourite house of Napoleon who visited it in 1810. By the end of the century, the house was selling almost 1 million bottles a year, but after 1875 family interest waned and the firm fell on harder times until bought by Léon de Tassigny, a broker, in 1920. In 1974 it was bought by the Chiquet family who have done a great deal to improve it. Although sales are only about one-third of those last century, Jacquesson is gaining in prestige. The wines are carefully made and partly fermented in oak. The house owns vineyards in some *grand* and *premier cru* villages. The style of wine is round and smooth and very easy to drink. Signature Brut is made from their own grapes only and fermented in oak, while their vintage Blanc de Blancs is a marvellously elegant and full-bodied wine.

68 rue du Colonel Fabien, 51530 Dizy, tel.: 26 55 68 11

KRUG

Founded in 1843 by Jean-Joseph Krug, who had first worked for Jacquesson and then married the English sister-in-law of Adolphe Jacquesson, Krug has always stood for uncompromising quality. It is a house with a dynasty making a very individual style of wine which, when young, may appear almost too austere, but which matures magnificently. Although they own some vineyards in excellent sites, and were lucky enough in the early 1970s to acquire the *monocru* of Le Mesnil, they do rely to some extent on carefully nurtured relationships with a number of growers. All their wines undergo the first fermentation in small oak, before being carefully blended. The policy here has always been to create a fine still wine before inducing the *prise de mousse*. Contrary to rumour, Krug is open to modernisation provided it does not spoil their wines' unique character. Stainless steel was tried but believed to change the style, and so was discarded.

Two generations always work together, so that the traditions are handed down smoothly. Today Henri Krug is working with Olivier, who will eventually take over. Although Krug feels very much a family business, in fact it was sold to Rémy during the 1970s, but the day-to-day running remains firmly in the family's hands. But the vineyard purchases made at that time were possible only because of the sale. Very recently control has passed to LVMH.

All the wines are serious, magnificent with food, and very different. The multi-vintage Grande Cuvée, first launched in 1979, is their flagship wine, very much a *cuvée de prestige*. Contrary to received wisdom, the house has always used a relatively large proportion of Meunier in its blends, although purchased from very special sites. They also make a Rosé structured enough to be drunk with meat dishes, a vintage when the year is good enough, and of course the Clos de Mesnil, again made in only the very best years.

5 rue Coquebert, 51051 Reims, tel.: 26 84 44 20

LANSON

An old house, founded in 1760 by François Delamotte, it remained in the total control of the Delamotte family until 1828 when Jean-Baptiste Lanson became associated with it. Nine years later his two nephews joined the business and, following the death of the Veuve Delamotte, the Lansons took control and changed the name of the firm to what we know today.

From 1926 onwards the firm made very considerable investments in the vineyards, holding in all 208 hectares in some of the most important villages. Sadly, following a series of takeovers, in 1991 LVMH, the then owners, sold the firm to Marne et Champagne but retained the Lanson vineyards. Clearly this has had a considerable effect on the style of the wine, notably that of the flagship Black Label.

Lanson Père et Fils, 12 boulevard Lundy, 51056 Reims, tel.: 26 78 50 50

LAURENT-PERRIER

Originally established in 1812 by the Laurent family, their son married a Mlle Perrier and on his death the widow added her name to his. She ran the company very successfully until her death in 1925 without an heir. It was bought in 1938 by Marie-Louise de Nonancourt and run by her son Bernard, who transformed it into one of the largest houses in the region. Having spent most of the war in the Resistance, he took over in 1948 and has created an elegant style of wine. The house runs 100 hectares of vineyard, but this is only a drop in the ocean of their needs which are mostly supplied by a network of small growers with whom the house works closely. It produces an elegant non-vintage wine, but also an excellent wine without any *dosage* called Ultra Brut, with sufficient fruit not to be over-austere. Their Rosé is one of the few to be made by fermenting on the skins to produce a genuinely pink wine, and they also make three very fine prestige *cuvées*; Grand Siècle with a high Chardonnay element which is very fine indeed, occasionally a Grand Siècle Exceptionnellement Millésimé, and finally the Grand Siècle Alexandra Brut Rosé.

Avenue de Champagne, 51150 Tours-sur-Marne, tel.: 26 58 91 22

LECLERC BRIANT

Founded in 1872, this is still a family-owned house making some very interesting wines. Pascal Leclerc, currently the head, has a number of single-vineyard sites, and likes to make wines which show the character of the soil. Thus he produces a number of special wines, such as Les Chèvres Pierreuses, from an individual vineyard. Another speciality is his Cuvée Rubis, a *rosé* champagne made from Pinot Noir fermented on the skins for up to five days, which produces a wine so dark that there was talk of it losing the *appellation* if made any deeper, but it certainly goes extremely well with food. A real individualist, M. Leclerc is an ardent salesman, and is also responsible for the new experimental easy-to-open cork.

67 rue de la Chaude-Ruelle, 51204 Epernay, tel.: 26 54 45 33

MAILLY GRAND CRU

Founded by Gabriel Simon in April 1929, this co-operative began with only twenty-four members and today has risen to seventy. It will be seventy years old in 1999, and its members own 70 hectares between them in the *grand cru* village. Production is deliberately limited to no more than 650,000 bottles in a year, and approximately half their sales go to export markets. A limited range of five *cuvées* only are made, a very elegant Brut Réserve, an Extra Brut, a special blend of old vintages, a Brut Vintage, a Rosé and finally a *cuvée de prestige*, Cuvée des Echansons, said to have an aroma of almonds and honey.

22 rue de la Libération, 51500 Mailly-Champagne, tel.: 26 49 41 10

MERCIER

This house was founded in 1858 by Eugène Mercier who combined five small houses into one with a head office address in Paris. A young man of only twenty at the time, he was a tremendous showman and probably did more than anyone else to market champagne to the population in general rather than just to the privileged few. It was he who built the amazing cellars in Epernay, designed from the very start to attract visitors. He was responsible for the creation of a great wine barrel which took twenty years to build and became a star turn at the 1889 Universal Exhibition in Paris. The construction of this cost the lives of the two coopers who worked closely with him on the project. One drowned while overseeing the bending of the staves, which were floated in Lake Balaton in Hungary, while the other died of exhaustion in 1881, on the day the work was completed. Their names were commemorated within the cask. Further excitement was caused when the Mercier balloon, moored at the 1900 Paris exhibition and offering a glass of champagne on board for visitors, broke away in a gust of wind and deposited its surprised passengers in Alsace, then in German hands!

During the 1950s the family invested in the Vallée de la Marne with plantings of mainly Pinot Meunier. In 1970 the company was acquired by Moët & Chandon and is therefore part of the LVMH group. Mercier has always specialised in wines of a wide commercial appeal, often far better than they are given credit for. The biggest-selling champagne in France, the NV wine tends to be full and rich with good ripe fruit. A speciality is the Demi-Sec, tasting of clean apple fruit and not cloying. Other styles include a vintage, a Rosé Brut, and a *cuvée de prestige*, Bulle d'Or, which contains more Chardonnay than the others.

20 avenue de Champagne, 51204 Epernay, tel.: 26 54 71 11

MOËT & CHANDON

Started by Claude Moët in 1743, Moët & Chandon is a dominant force in the region. Set on its road to fame by the friendship of

Jean-Rémy Moët and Napoleon, it also controls today Mercier and Ruinart, while both Veuve Clicquot (and therefore Canard-Duchêne) and Pommery are part of the LVMH group and Krug has very recently been acquired. Despite its growth in the nineteenth century, its standing slipped during the early years of this century, and it was rescued by the remarkable Robert-Jean de Vogüé, who among his other operations persuaded his board of directors to sanction the first Dom Pérignon wine in spite of the depression of the time, the first shipments leaving Moët's cellars in 1935. What is remarkable about Moët's operation is its sheer scale, and the quality that they continue to achieve particularly in the basic Brut Imperial, which shows such excellent fruit, year in, year out. The vintage wines always show the character of the year, even if they tend to be released a little on the early side, but there is never any doubt of the quality of the Dom Pérignon wines, with a strong, steely backbone and plenty of warm fruit.

20 avenue de Champagne, 51333 Epernay, tel.: 26 51 20 00

G. H. MUMM

Another house started by German immigrants in 1827. The Mumm family made the mistake of never becoming French citizens, which led to the confiscation of the house after the First World War. The syndicate which purchased it was led by René Lalou until 1973. He bought control of Perrier-Jouët in 1959, but ten years later Seagram took a stake in the business and finally in 1985 took control of the Mumm group, which by now also included Heidsieck Monopole. Its leading brand is, of course, Cordon Rouge, which was introduced last century by their Paris agent who thought that putting the sash of the Légion d'Honneur on the bottle might well help to increase its sales. This is an acceptable, if slightly bland, champagne, but Mumm does have a range of prestige *cuvées*. The great *blanc de blancs* once known as Crémant de Cramant now has to be called Mumm de Cramant, but still shows the slightly lighter sparkle for which it is famous; René Lalou is a more powerful vintage wine, based on 50 per cent Pinot Noir with Chardonnay, all coming from 100 per cent *crus*, while a third, Grand Cordon, was introduced in 1991. Recently Seagrams sold both Mumm and Perrier-Jouët to Hicks, Muse, Tate & Furst.

29/34 rue du Champs-de-Mars, 51053 Reims, tel.: 26 49 59 69

BRUNO PAILLARD

One of the great success stories of post-war Champagne, it was founded in 1981 by Bruno Paillard, himself a young and energetic broker. His premises are in a new temperature-controlled building made of glass and steel, and the whole business is thoroughly modern and efficient, but absolutely dedicated to quality.

The styles include the NV Première Cuvée Brut made from the first pressing of all three grapes, the Première Cuvée Brut Rosé, a Blanc de Blancs and a vintage. Elegance, freshness and fruitiness are hallmarks of these champagnes, all of which are *brut* in style. Very interestingly, the date of disgorgement is given on the bottles. The house is wholly owned by Bruno Paillard. However, he is also the largest shareholder in a publicly owned group, Boizel-Chanoine. This group includes the houses of Boizel, Abel Lepitre, De Venoge, Alexandre Bonnet and in 1998 acquired Philipponnat.

Avenue de Champagne, 51100 Reims, tel.: 26 36 20 22

JOSEPH PERRIER

This, the one major champagne house situated in Châlons, was founded by Joseph Perrier in 1825 but sold to the Pithois family, who still own it, before the end of the century. Its premises had the dubious distinction of being used as the HQ of the *Führer* of Champagne during the German occupation of the Second World War.

Now run by Claude Fourmon, the son of Jean-Claude Fourmon the colleague of the Red Marquis, Robert-Jean de Vogüé, it remains a relatively small house, once a member of the now dissolved Syndicat des Grandes Marques, making excellent but undervalued champagnes. If the basic non-vintage Cuvée Royale is a straight-forward blend of the three grape varieties, to be enjoyed in an uncomplicated manner, the vintage wines, and most notably the prestige wine, Cuvée Josephine, are all very fine wines indeed. The 1985 Cuvée Josephine, still available in magnums for the Millennium, has a real depth of ripeness and maturity. Definitely a house to follow.

69 avenue de Paris, 51005 Châlons-sur-Marne, tel.: 26 68 29 51

PERRIER-JOUËT

In 1811, the uncle of Joseph Perrier started this house, Jouët being his wife's maiden name. By 1815 the wine was being shipped to Britain and then, twenty years later, to the USA. It has always been a favourite in English-speaking markets. Following the death of Charles Perrier, it passed into the hands of a nephew, and in 1934 to the Budin family, related by marriage. Although sold in 1959 to Mumm, the family still run it, and in 1970 launched on to the market their prestige wine sold in the famous art nouveau bottle. Perrier-Jouët has superb vineyards particularly in the Côte des Blancs at Avize and Cramant, as well as at Mailly, Aÿ and Dizy, but in spite of these holdings needs to buy almost 60 per cent of its grapes on the open market. Its top wines are the rich Blason de France, which is also made in a *rosé* style, and the Chardonnay-dominated Belle Epoque, an elegant, rich, toasty and complex wine. Recently sold, with Mumm, to Hicks, Muse, Tate & Furst.

28 avenue de Champagne, 51201 Epernay, tel.: 26 53 38 00

PHILIPPONNAT

A relatively modern house, founded only in 1912, when the family, who had been growers in the Vallée de la Marne for several centuries, moved into Mareuil-sur-Aÿ. In 1935 Philipponnat bought 5.5 hectares of vines at Mareuil in the largest walled vineyard in Champagne, the Clos des Goisses. The house was acquired first by Gosset in 1980 and then, in 1987, it passed to the control of the Marie Brizard group. In 1998, after considerable negotiations, it was bought by Bruno Paillard.

These wines are made in a very traditional style and go well with food. They also have a less aggressive mousse than many. The NV is dominated by Pinot Noir, normally 70 per cent, with the first fermentation in wood. The Brut Rosé is creamy and elegant, while the Clos des Goisses is an intense, complex wine with strong, ripe fruit, capable of long ageing, when it acquires the aroma and flavour of toasted hazelnuts.

13 rue du Pont, 51160 Mareuil-sur-Aÿ, tel.: 26 56 93 00

PLOYEZ-JACQUEMART

This small, but highly thought-of house, was started in 1930 by Marcel Ployez and his wife, née Jacquemart. Today it is run by Gérard Ployez and his daughter, Laurence, who is now the winemaker. They own a vineyard situated at the top of the property, but this accounts for only a tiny proportion of the grapes, most of which are purchased from good sites in the Valley of the Marne and the Côte des Blancs. Very fine makers, although on a small scale, their basic wines are Extra Quality Brut, Vintage Brut, usually mostly Chardonnay, a Blanc de Blancs, and a barrel-fermented prestige wine of great interest made from the two Pinot grapes only, called Cuvée Liesse d'Hardonville.

Ludes, 51500 Rilly-la-Montagne, tel.: 26 61 11 87

POL ROGER

A family-owned firm still, it was founded in 1849 by Pol Roger, and was well established by 1900 when the name of the Roger family was changed to Pol-Roger, by which they are still known. Probably the most famous member of the family was Maurice, Mayor of Epernay when it was occupied for seven days in 1914. His stand against the Germans, who threatened to kill him and torch the town, is legendary. Today the firm is run by two great-grandsons of the founder, Christian de Billy and Christian Pol-Roger. Long a favourite champagne on the British market, its most famous devotee was Winston Churchill, for whom they created the Imperial Pint bottle (alas no longer allowed by the European Union) because although he felt that a half was insufficient, his wife, Clementine, would get cross if he drank a whole bottle. 'I saw him many times the better for it, but never the worse,' commented his daughter, Lady Soames. Cuvée Sir Winston Churchill is their prestige wine, named after their famous customer. Although originally very much a Pinot-dominated style, in recent years the Chardonnay has appeared to dominate, but the wines still show the amazing clarity and very fine bubbles for which the house is well known. The White Foil non-vintage wine is an assemblage of all three grapes in equal proportions, and they also make *rosé* and vintage wines. Their Blanc de Chardonnay vintage is one of the finest of its kind, with elegance, length and liveliness, and also with the capacity to age. The Sir Winston Churchill is a very big wine, but its blend is never disclosed, although it clearly has a high Pinot Noir content and is a wine for long ageing.

1 rue Henri Lelarge, 51206 Epernay, tel.: 26 59 58 00

POMMERY & GRENO

Founded in 1836 by M. Greno, it became known as Pommery & Greno when a M. Pommery was taken aboard as a partner. Two years later, on his death, his widow took command of the firm. Another of the great ladies for which this area is so famous, Mme Pommery was one of the first to realise the potential of the old chalk cellars, and extended hers by buying from the Ruinarts and turning them into a real showpiece, as indeed she did with the mock gothic castle above them. It is claimed this was Mme Pommery's tribute to her British customers and was supposed to be built in the 'Scottish baronial' style. But she was a very shrewd businesswoman, again devoted to quality and determined to produce the finest, most delicate and, interestingly, driest possible wines, and she certainly concentrated hard on the British market. At the same time, she saw the need to own vineyards and managed to buy some 300 hectares in fine areas. After her death the company gradually slipped into a decline, although her daughter had married into the de Polignac family. Bought out in 1979 and sold again in 1983, the firm's current winemaker is Prince Alain de Polignac, who has transformed the wines, although since purchase by LVMH in 1990 it has appeared as if volume is being sought. The basic NV wine, the Brut Royal, is a classic blend, sometimes a little on the light side, and occasionally released too young. However, the vintage wines show real fruit and length, while the Cuvée Louise Pommery, the house's Chardonnay-based prestige wine, is delicious, light, fresh and yet quite capable of long life – a real gem. Pommery have just introduced two new wines to the range: Summertime, a *blanc de blancs* for summer drinking, available only from June to August each year, and a Brut Royal Apanage, designed as an aperitif or first-course wine.

5 place du Général Gouraud, 51053 Reims, tel.: 26 61 62 63

LOUIS ROEDERER

Another family-owned house which takes its name from its founder who came from Strasbourg to help his uncle Nicolas Schreider. Six years later, Louis Roederer inherited the business. The house has always been noted for producing great quality, and today it is among the most profitable. Its foundations were laid last century by the first Louis who understood the importance of the export markets, particularly in the USA and then Russia. The great Cristal wine was first made for the Tsar and his court. It was then very sweet, which created a serious problem when stocks held for the Russian market had to be sold elsewhere after the 1917 Revolution. Roederer has sufficient vineyards to provide most of the grapes needed. In 1975 Jean-Claude Rouzaud, the current head of the house, took control after the death of his grandmother. The Roederer wines have got even finer, partly because M. Rouzaud, a winemaker himself, believes firmly in making the best possible wine before considering the bubbles. Although fermented in small stainless steel vats, the reserve wines are all kept in large oak barrels. Brut Premier is the non-vintage blend, powerful, honeyed and long, and based primarily on the Pinot Noir. Vintage wines are made in the best years, but undoubtedly the Cristal, now dry in style but still sold in the clear bottle, is a fine, full, rich and yet elegant wine, much sought after in spite of its price.

21 boulevard Lundy, 51053 Reims, tel.: 26 40 42 11

RUINART PÈRE & FILS

This is the oldest of the champagne houses, started in 1729 by Nicolas Ruinart, nephew of Dom Ruinart, winemaker and friend of Dom Pérignon. The firm of Gosset can claim to be older, but not in terms of making sparkling wines. The house prospered under Napoleon, although the royalist sympathies of Irénée Ruinart were displayed when he welcomed Charles X to Reims at the time of his coronation. Despite its premises being virtually destroyed during the bombardment suffered between 1914 and 1916, the firm continued to prosper as a family concern until sold to Moët & Chandon in 1963. Still run independently, Ruinart has a special style of its own, very rich yet elegant at the same time. Its most famous wine is the vintage Dom Ruinart, a superb *blanc de blancs*, owing its richness to the Chardonnay grown on the Montagne de Reims, and the house has just launched its new 'R' de Ruinart *rosé* in a replica of the eighteenth-century Ruinart Chardonnay bottle.

4 rue des Crayères, 51053 Reims, tel.: 26 77 51 51

SALON

This is the only house which produces just one style of champagne, a vintage Blanc de Blancs. It was the creation of Eugène-Aimé Salon who was born into a grower's family in 1867. He first became a teacher and later made a fortune as a furrier (and a politician) in Paris. In 1911, he bought a vineyard in Le Mesnil-sur-Oger with the intention of making a perfect champagne from Chardonnay, purely for the enjoyment of himself and his friends. In 1921, pressurised by demand, he finally applied for a commercial licence and Salon, as a house, was born. He began to buy grapes from other growers in Le Mesnil, but only accepted the very best and made his wine from *cuvée* juice only. Only in the finest vintages was Salon sold under his label, the wine being sold off in the years which did not meet his exacting standards. During the 1920s Salon became the house champagne of Maxim's. M. Salon died in 1943.

In the last 72 years Salon has only released 29 vintages.

Besserat de Bellefon acquired Salon in 1963, but in 1989 it was bought by Laurent-Perrier, returning once again to the control of a family firm. The winemaking is very traditional, with grapes selected from the same vineyards chosen by M. Salon, and apparently still in the same proportions that he stipulated. There is no malolactic and the wines are aged in wood. *Dégorgement à la volée* is still practised and the wines are matured for between eight and ten years before release. The most striking aspect of flavour in these wines is that of hazelnuts or walnuts appearing through great richness of fruit, but with a striking level of acidity which keeps the wine fresh.

51190 Le Mesnil-sur-Oger, Avize, tel.: 26 57 51 65

JACQUES SELOSSE

A highly interesting grower of powerful wines, all made from Chardonnay, with the exception of the *rosé*, and showing their chalk soil in the taste. The first fermentation is with grapes that have been carefully sorted, and takes place in oak. Unusually for the region, these are left on their lees for up to six months, being stirred up on a regular basis as might be done with a great white Burgundy. Equally unusual is the use of a *solera* system for the reserve wine; each year one-third of the reserve wine is used in the NV blend and replaced by wine from that vintage. The result is a reserve wine of intriguing weight and complexity. The wines are given a very long ageing, up to seven or eight years before being hand-disgorged. Beautifully balanced wines, they are very different.

Styles of wine made are a Tradition Brut NV, a very dry wine of considerable richness, a *sec* (Cuvée Exquise), and Extra Brut Blanc de Blancs, Vintage and a Cuvée Prestige.

61 rue Ernest Vallé, 51190 Avize, tel.: 26 50 53 56

TAITTINGER

Although this house can trace its origins back to 1743 when it was started by Jacques Fourneaux, for all practical purposes it was founded in 1930 by Pierre Taittinger, and has, since the last war, become one of the largest and most important houses in Champagne, owning the historic Château de la Marquetterie, kept nowadays for special events. All through its rapid expansion, the firm has kept purchasing vineyards and its current holdings, which account for about half the grapes needed, are on some fine sites in both the Montagne de Reims and the Côte des Blancs. The current, very dynamic chairman is Claude Taittinger, and the wines tend to be fresh, lively and elegant. The NV wines are all disgorged after mechanical *remuage*, but their prestige Comtes de Champagne, which may be *blanc de blancs* or *rosé*, are riddled by hand and show elegance and some good biscuity characters. Despite their apparent lightness they can and do benefit from long ageing. They also produce their Collection champagnes, which are all vintage wines sold in bottles which have been decorated by different artists. Collection is certainly an excellent name, for long after the wine has been drunk, the bottles themselves give a great deal of pleasure.

Taittinger are the parent company to Irroy and vastly overshadow its elegant, Chardonnay-dominated Brut NV. Irroy also makes a subtle and stylish *rosé*.

9 place Saint-Nicaise, 51061 Reims, tel.: 26 85 45 45

DE VENOGE

Famously described by Henry Vizetelly in 1882 as 'the great Epernay manufacturer of common-class champagne', the house was originally established as Mareuil-sur-Aÿ in 1837 but moved to Epernay two years later. De Venoge has never aspired to produce great classic champagnes, but rather decent, well-made and good-value wines. Acquired in 1958 by the Troillard family, it has had a chequered career, particularly during the early 1980s when its stocks became seriously depleted. However, since 1986 when Thierry Mantoux became Managing Director, the overall image and quality have improved. A change in packaging together with easy-to-drink and fruity styles, have given the wines a strong consumer appeal.

Their NV Cordon Bleu Brut, based heavily on Pinot Noir, is round, creamy and ripe. Interestingly, this house produces a Blanc de Noirs, a vintage Blanc de Blancs as well as a standard blend, and the Princesse Rosé, very pale and based on Chardonnay, and a Blanc de Blancs Prestige Cuvée.

30 avenue de Champagne, 51204 Epernay, tel.: 26 55 01 01

VEUVE CLICQUOT PONSARDIN

Although founded by Philippe Clicquot in 1772, this house owed its swift rise to his daughter-in-law, the famous Veuve Clicquot, who sublimated her grief at her beloved husband's early death by building up one of the most prestigious firms in Champagne. Apart from the development of *remuage* and the *pupitre*, she was to prove very astute in picking her employees, from Antoine Müller onwards, including M. Bohne who opened up the Russian market for her, and finally Edmond Werlé, to whom she eventually left the business on her death in 1866. It remained with the descendants of M. Werlé until 1985, when it merged with Henriot, only to be taken over eventually by LVMH. It is still run as a separate enterprise, and holds some 285 hectares of vineyards, barely enough to supply one-third of the company's needs. The style of the wines has always been fairly rich, even the Brut NV, or Yellow Label, which depends heavily on Pinot Noir with a reasonable amount of

Meunier too. Good use of reserve wines and a dash of Chardonnay, however, prevent it from being too heavy. La Grande Dame, the vintage prestige *cuvée*, is a magnificent wine, rich, ripe and round, but also with a nice lift of acidity and a touch of hazelnuts, while their vintage Reserve always manages to show the character of the particular year. Known colloquially, certainly in the City of London, as 'the Widow', these wines have always had a great following.

12 rue du Temple, 51054 Reims, tel.: 26 89 54 40

VILMART

A small grower founded in 1890, it has 11 hectares of Pinot Noir and Chardonnay in a *premier cru* village, which are grown on an organic basis, a fact of which René Champs and his son Laurent are very proud, believing that by using a natural environment they increase the flavour of their grapes. René Champs came into the champagne trade by virtue of marrying Mlle Vilmart. Before that he had been a carpenter and very fine furniture maker, and the stained-glass windows in the cellars are of his creation, self-taught. All the wines are fermented in oak casks, the majority large, old *foudres*. The wines remain on the lees for a considerable time before being disgorged. The Champs, father and son, are convinced that mechanical *remuage* gives their wines a cleaner finish, but hand *remuage* is still used for smaller and larger sizes. Their basic non-vintage wine, the Grande Réserve, is an easy-to-drink, rounded and fruity wine, but the Grand Cellier is definitely more complex, while the Grand Cellier d'Or, the vintage wine, is rich and honeyed, with a touch of baking bread and spices in the aroma. Among their new wines is their Cœur de Cuvée, made from the very best part of the *cuvée*, and a special wine designed for the Millennium made from the 1990 vintage is sold in a clear glass bottle bearing a design by M. Champs, reminiscent of his beloved stained-glass windows.

4 rue de la République, 51500 Rilly-la-Montagne, tel.: 26 48 40 01

VRANKEN-LAFITTE

This firm was established by a Belgian, Paul-François Vranken, as late as 1976. Initially, its business was supplying BOB champagnes, but M. Vranken saw the opportunity of selling his own label, Veuve Monnier. A fairly average champagne, it nevertheless sold well in France and, after the appointment of a M. Charles Lafitte to the company's board, a second higher-quality brand was launched under that name. A further brand known as Demoiselle made a trio and this house now has a large number of labels. Recently, Vranken has acquired the Bouzy house of Barancourt. On the whole, the quality under all the labels tends to be average; however, the Charles Lafitte include NV Brut and Demi-Sec, a very nice Rosé and vintage styles. Since 1994 the house has owned Barancourt.

BP3 Bouzy, 51150 Tours-sur-Marne, tel.: 26 59 50 50

16

Storing and Serving Champagne

It cannot be gainsaid that today most bottles of champagne are bought on impulse. The arrival of easily available, usually inexpensive champagnes in every supermarket and high-street wine shop helped to create a situation where, as in France, many began to expect to buy as the fancy took them, or to buy a bottle to take as a gift. And the question was increasingly asked: could champagne, and in particular the non-vintage wines, be kept?

A good many years have passed since any merchant importing supplies of champagne would automatically place an order for the anticipated demand three or even six months in advance, to avoid selling to customers wines which had been shaken up by travelling. The wines arrived and were carefully laid down to recover before being offered for sale.

Today, faced with the need to maximise profits, this is no longer possible. The wine will be ordered according to need, cleared from bond and put straight on the shelves – a fact which, in part, accounts for the often-heard complaints about varying quality in a chosen favourite. If the previous purchase had been made from stock landed six to nine months previously and the current purchase from newly arrived stock, the difference can be very marked. Additionally, many of the less expensive bottles will have been made for swift sale and not for the longer lees ageing given to more expensive wines, and will hardly have been rested between receiving the final *dosage* and being dressed for sale and transportation. Wines such as these can indeed taste very harsh and raw, in need of time to rest and, for want of a better word, recuperate, to show at their best.

Therefore, wherever possible, impulse buying should be shunned and the wine bought well in advance of the expected date of opening. This particularly applies to the inexpensive wines, and less so if the purchase is made from a fine-wine merchant, but some resting period between purchase and opening is really always preferable.

Champagne can, of course, be kept. Although good makers disgorge and release wine only when they feel it to be ready, maturity is always a matter of personal taste. In general terms the British like their champagnes more mature than the French, but obviously this does not apply to everyone. Indeed, life would be far easier if a date of, say, disgorgement formed part of the label information, but that is not generally the case at present. But given the desire to mature champagne, whether vintage or non-vintage, there are certain conditions which should be observed.

In the cellars in Champagne, the bottles lie ageing in a stable temperature of about 10°C (50°F) which does not vary in summer or winter. Few private houses these days have true cellars, but to keep wine it is better to have a coolish temperature which remains even. If warmer than the ideal, the wine will simply age a little faster, but at all costs extremes of temperature should be avoided. The bottles should be stored ideally in absolute darkness, since exposure to light destroys wine, and they should be in an area free from any vibration – not too close to a main road used by heavy lorries, for example.

Finally, in the case of champagne, there is the problem of whether to store them horizontally or vertically. Received wisdom for years has been that wine, including sparkling wine, should always be laid on its side to prevent the cork drying out. However, about ten years ago word trickled through from California that for sparkling wine it was perfectly safe to store the bottles upright. At first little notice was taken of this, especially in Champagne itself, but it is now held to be correct, since the head space between the wine and cork is not empty but filled with an inert gas, carbon dioxide, and this acts as a buffer protecting the wine in the unlikely event of the cork drying out. The current belief would therefore seem to be: look at the storage space available and decide which stance would make better use of it.

There is an art to opening a champagne bottle safely. Obviously if the cork is encouraged to leap out of the bottle uncontrolled, especially in an enclosed area such as a dining room, it can do considerable damage – to eyes and ears, not to mention ceilings and walls. The pressure within a bottle of 72 pounds per square inch is not to be trifled with, despite the example set by Formula One racing drivers.

The bottle should be moved as little as possible and certainly never shaken about. If a journey is inevitable, then thirty minutes in a domestic freezer will help to stabilise the mousse. But normally chilling in an ice bucket or refrigerator will help to reduce pressure slightly, making the process easier. Stand the bottle upright and remove the foil. Then the wire muzzle should be unscrewed, keeping a thumb over the cork at all times. Remove the muzzle and capsule, and, holding the cork firmly, turn the bottle but not the cork. At this point it is helpful to hold the bottle at a slight angle, tilted away from any people close by. The cork should emerge quietly, with a very slight sound sometimes described as 'the sigh of a satisfied woman'. The tilting prevents loss of wine as the mousse is released. Careful handling is absolutely essential to prevent flying corks inflicting nasty injuries,

However, this art could be overtaken by events. Two houses, Leclerc Briant and Cattier, have collaborated in the design of an easier-to-handle cork. Following considerable research it was found that elderly folk and some women found the removal of the cork so difficult that even when presented as a gift, the bottle would remain unopened. This new cork aims to prevent this problem and is currently being test-marketed. It is based on a spigot which releases the pressure, with a gentle hiss, enabling the cork then to be removed easily. It remains to be seen whether this invention has major appeal, but certainly a number of Leclerc Briant's customers like it very much, and it has been featured on French television and in London broadsheet newspapers. Only the future will tell whether its prospects are long-term.

Tasting different champagnes is an excellent way to discover preferred wines or styles, but this is usually left to professionals, such as makers, buyers and journalists, who are looking for either intrinsic quality, or wines to buy or recommend. But it is always fascinating to hold a tasting for consumers, to hear their comments and learn about their preferences, because serious champagne drinkers do taste most conscientiously.

At this point, the choice of glasses becomes extremely important. Firstly, the glass should, if possible, be similar to what the taster normally uses, since a change of shape can radically alter the view of a wine. Secondly, whether for tasting or sipping, the glass should be clear and bright, but without any trace of a detergent which will make any wine fall flat and dull, and sparkling wine lose its mousse very swiftly.

Champagne glasses: the flute, ISO design and Paris goblet

The classic champagne glass is the flute, which is not, as is often supposed, a modern invention. The flute's shape enables the steady rise of a central column of delicate bubbles to be seen and admired. Bubbles, to show off their best, do like an uneven base from which to rise. It gives them something to cling to; so, unless the glass is hand-blown, it can be worth marking the base with a scratch from the stem and a short way up the inside of the bowl to encourage the mousse. The ISO design, brilliant for most tasting, does not seem to enhance sparkling wines of any type, and neither does the ubiquitous Paris goblet. The notorious coupe, once used so often at weddings and parties, is also not suitable. The width and shallowness of the bowl destroys the bubbles very swiftly, results in the wine warming up very fast and losing its liveliness, and certainly neutralises any possible aroma. It is an old design, however, originating during the seventeenth century, and the most famous is now preserved in the Antique Porcelain Company in the USA, said to be modelled on the breasts of Marie Antoinette. It is certainly a shape more suited to White Lady cocktails than to elegant sparkling wines.

Whether for tasting or sipping, the wine in the glass should be clear and bright. A *blanc de blancs* style or a very young wine should be pale, with maybe a delicate green light, while any wine with a high Pinot content will tend to be more golden. Watch the bubbles. They should be very fine – a sign of careful second fermentation – and rise steadily to the surface, not only when just poured but for a long time after. Candidates for induction into the most senior of the Champagne wine orders, the Ordre des Coteaux de la Champagne, have to face its committee and be instructed in the method of tasting. After looking at the effervescence, they are allowed to nose the aroma – lively, fruity, with toasty or biscuity character sometimes showing hazelnuts or apples or even honey. Then they are asked to hear the wine – in other words, to listen to the rush of the bubbles to the surface. Finally they are asked to taste the wine and feel the effect on the palate – the gentle fizz, not too violent in a fine wine, which lifts the aromas and flavours in the mouth, producing the unique taste sensations of champagne and the length and breadth of it. The wine should sing.

Many people are puzzled by the different bottle sizes, most of which have biblical names. No one appears to know the origin of these names, not even in Champagne itself. Serena Sutcliffe postulates that possibly they arose from the fact that, once upon a time, the bottle manufacturers were predominantly Jewish, but admits that this is simply flying a kite. The sizes in which the wine may be sold are currently as follows.

Quarter bottle	18.7 cl.
Half bottle	37.5 cl.
Bottle	75 cl.
Magnum (double bottle/2 bottles)	150 cl.
Jeroboam (double magnum/4 bottles)	300 cl.

Most houses do make all these sizes, from half to magnum, and usually, though not always, jeroboams as well. Quarters, or splits for airlines, are not made in the bottle but are decanted under pressure from magnums into the quarters. The next five sizes are made to order and decanted into these sizes.

Rehoboam	(triple magnum/6 bottles)
Methuselah	(8 bottles)
Salmanazar	(12 bottles)
Balthazar	(16 bottles)
Nebuchadnezzar	(20 bottles)

It is important to remember when buying different sizes what the effect of decanting will be. Firstly, air will have been able to affect the wine, thus adding to oxidation; secondly, the pressure in the final bottle will be slightly less. Quarters and splits on aeroplanes are usually presented with screw tops. Half bottles are usually made in the same way as bottles. They tend to age rather faster than bottles, or than magnums which are said to be the perfect size for slow ageing, but this view is vigorously contested at Krug, where it is believed that the size of the bottle matters less than the strength and character of the wine. The sizes larger than Jeroboam are only produced to order and are not normally available.

The temperature at which champagne is served is all-important. It needs to be chilled well, but not too cold, at something between 6 to 8°C. This may be achieved by leaving the bottle for several hours in a refrigerator, or by placing it in an ice bucket filled with a mixture of water and ice cubes. If in a hurry, add some salt as well, as this lowers the temperature even more, or invest in some quick-cooling jackets, easily obtainable as Rapid Ice. The problem with the latter is that the top couple of inches of the bottle tends to be warmer than the rest. In really cold weather, simply leaving the bottles outside will produce the best temperature.

On opening, the wine will have a powerful mousse, unless it has very considerable age, and the best way to fill a glass is to pour a small amount, let the fizz settle and then top up. Unlike most wines which should never fill more than one-third of the glass, champagne poured into a flute can fill it up to within about 1 inch of the top. Look, and enjoy the clarity and bubbles; nose and relish the aromas of breadiness, or fruit and honey; taste and enjoy the sensation. *Santé*, as the makers would say.

17

The Future of Champagne

As the Millennium approaches, Champagne obviously stands at a crossroads. It is a highly desired wine, made from a restricted area and only three grape varieties. The region has a difficult climate, ameliorated by a unique chalky soil – reasons, possibly, why the very best are such elegant and potentially long-lived wines. The twentieth century has seen it suffer many difficulties: the aftermath of the phylloxera, riots and wars. Regarded as a luxury, it is vulnerable to economic difficulties during any form of depression, whether in France or in the all-important export markets. Finally it has, for the very first time, to compete with increasingly better-made sparkling wines from other parts of the world, where favourable climatic conditions make the cost of the grapes considerably cheaper. And although the total amount produced at present in these other regions is only a small percentage of that from Champagne, it clearly represents a potential challenge, a fact not lost on those houses who invested in sparkling-wine production in other areas.

There is little that Champagne can do about the delimited area and therefore production levels. While there are proponents of expanding the area under vine, and Claude Taittinger is among them, it is difficult to see how this could come about in any comprehensive way. When the area was originally mapped out, it is true that there were landowners with suitable soils who refused the *appellation* because, at that time, it offered a fragile source of income, but even if the commission charged with looking at soil structures accepted these hectares, it would be only a drop in the ocean. It is also true that there are a handful of areas which might just be expanded by serious terracing, but again these numbers are relatively minute. Any repeat of the horrendous over-production created by demand during the 1980s has been effectively blocked by new laws limiting yield to just over 10,000 kilos per hectare, a figure which will not necessarily be reached in every year anyhow, (1997, for example). So it would seem on all fronts that increasing the amount of champagne made on an annual basis is not likely unless the new laws are repealed. However, after the scare of the early 1990s, and with the new accent on quality at all levels, this does not seem feasible at present.

The question therefore arises: should Champagne try to produce quantity? Would it not make more sense to establish the wines of this region as in the top range for quality instead? Given the production costs of good grapes in this difficult climate, there is a case to be made for such a decision, but how could it be implemented? There is no doubt that at the very top level Champagne is unique in its style and elegance, but there are many wines which fall short of this greatness. They are certainly all made within AOC regulations, but often to the minimum standard laid down. In the German Rheingau, the association known as Charta is composed of makers of Rheingau Riesling of a standard far higher than that required by the German Wine Law of 1971. To a certain extent the old Society of Grandes Marques tried to do the same, but the failure of its members to accept the new draft regulations means that at present there is no such body to speak for Champagne with one voice. Yet probably the only way to increase the quality of champagne wines across the board is to tighten the AOC regulations. Much has been already done. A reduction in yields in the vineyards and the amount of juice derived from the pressing, and a longer ageing process, are all moves in the right direction. Yet it cannot be done too quickly without affecting large amounts of people relying on champagne for their livelihood.

A major problem currently concerns pricing policies which have led to serious difficulties for many houses. While those at the top with great names are doing very well, it is an open secret that there are many who are not. A stagnant domestic market has put pressure on prices. Since two out of every three bottles of champagne sold is on the French market, failure here will lead to problems. In a nutshell, many growers and co-operatives are selling wines at a heavily discounted price. While this does not affect top names, it does prevent many middle-range makers increasing their prices to a commercial level which reflects their quality, thus seriously affecting their profitability

However, at the time of writing it is apparent that, with the Millennium approaching, some growers are leaving their wines to lie *sur lattes* in anticipation of a considerable rise in price. Considering the catastrophe in the early 1990s, this is a very short-sighted strategy with possibly destructive consequences at the lower-priced end of the market.

Although the recovery in export shipments so marked during 1996 appears to be continuing strongly, the stagnation of the domestic market is causing great concern, particularly to the co-operatives and smaller houses or growers, who tend to rely heavily on that market. Since the agreement on stabilisation of grape prices to last until the Millennium, the old unease between different sections of the trade has resurfaced. During the late 1980s, when grape prices soared apparently out of control, and now with the new agreement fixing prices at a slightly higher level than most makers would like, many in Champagne feel that although it is likely that such measures could stabilise the price of the wines and therefore breathe new life into the market, at the same time this agreement could be designed to push smaller producers out of business in order to rationalise the industry. Certainly, although the set price is one or two francs per kilo of grapes above the figure preferred by most, the top exporting firms are able to absorb this discrepancy, particularly if they have a number of brands under an umbrella company, like LVMH, or if, like Louis Roederer and Bollinger, they have large vineyard holdings. However, some smaller houses are undoubtedly suffering financial hardship, particularly where the vast majority of their grapes has to be purchased. On the other hand, this situation could strengthen the position of the co-operatives and the grower-makers, to whom the purchase of grapes is not an issue.

Conspiracy theories are nothing new to Champagne. Indeed, they have been part of the many crises to affect the area since 1890. If there is any truth in them this time, it is easy to see how the agreement on prices might benefit some of the large *negociant* houses being accused, by rumour at any rate, of giving in too easily to the new price structure. Smaller houses falling by the wayside would reduce the demand for grapes, enabling larger concerns to buy more and therefore almost certainly drive the price per kilo downwards in the long run, thus increasing their all-important profitability. But equally such a move would reduce growers' incomes and might well result in an increase of grower champagnes available, if history were to be repeated, thus polarising production and destroying much of the middle range.

In such a case, the surviving great houses would probably be able to raise levels of quality by selecting only the best grapes, as greater choice would be available. It might also then be possible to reduce still further either the permitted yield per hectare or the amount of juice taken from a *marc* of 4,000 kilos.

But the major strength of Champagne has always been the range of styles and prices available – something for everyone, so to speak – and such a scenario would be bound to create a large price gap between the top wines and the inexpensive ones. Yet one of the problems which will almost certainly arise next century is the ever-improving sparkling wines from notably the New World, with Australia, New Zealand, South Africa, South America, California and Oregon all producing most often from the same grape varieties and by the same method. Some of these wines already compete in the market with the inexpensive BOB champagnes, and even with some of the aggressively marketed well-known middle-range brands. In these circumstances, to destroy a strong range of middle-priced names could prove self-destructive.

Some form of rationalisation may well be needed, and one great example of a system that might work is Champagne Barancourt. In this instance three families merged their vineyards in 1969 to create the Domaine de Barancourt, the three sons having earlier joined together to purchase some land deserted after phylloxera in order to have sufficient vineyard holdings to make the venture possible. Today Barancourt has a high reputation for its wines, and can supply about 90 per cent of the grapes it needs, with holdings in the *grand cru* villages of Bouzy, Ambonnay and Cramant, and the 99 per cent *premier cru* Tauxières among others. Undoubtedly other such ventures could be established and might help to raise the image of quality so vital to the future.

But whether in viticulture, winemaking or marketing, there is no doubt that the Champagne region has to decide its future direction. If it is to remain unique, rather than becoming merely *primus inter pares*, then the major move must be towards quality. Of course there are laws in place which should secure this but, as with all AOC areas, the rules lay down no more than a minimum standard, and many wines are made to just that: the lowest permitted quality. At this point, sadly, other countries can now offer equivalent or sometimes better value. This is a new development, and it is therefore immensely unfortunate that at this particular juncture the members of the Syndicat des Grandes Marques have been unable to agree on a draft series of technical and commercial measures to ensure the absolute top quality in their members' wines. This would have lit a torch for quality illuminating the way into the twenty-first century.

In terms of overall production, there has not yet been any serious challenge to the pre-eminence of Champagne, but this will certainly alter over the next twenty years or so as new plantings for sparkling wines reach maturity in other countries. This fact has surely been recognised in the region and by all those houses, among many of the most prestigious names, who have invested money, time and expertise in making fine sparkling wines in the New World. Whether acting overtly, or in some cases covertly, they would seem to have recognized a growing market for such wines which one day Champagne, with its strict geographical limitations, will no longer be able to satisfy.

Currently the marketing of brands appears to be either via price-cutting to achieve volume sales, or by repositioning wines at the premium end of the market. This is a ploy that can be used well by the major groups such as Rémy, LVMH or Seagram. Many houses, however, are not in this happy position, particularly those which remain family-owned, and for whom the choice at present is hard. The PR arm of the CIVC has recently become much more active. There is little doubt that the sheer scale of the market collapse of 1990 has made an impact, and much more attention than ever before is being paid to the need to explain policy to both the wine trade overseas and the consumer. The latest idea is a booklet, appearing over several editions, which divides champagnes into different classes – heart, soul, body or spirit – and asks consumers to choose the style they feel suits the wine they are drinking. This is a novel idea, and certainly provides *aficionados* with a basis for discussion over a bottle, but its real importance lies in the change of attitude to the market, and the realisation that the customer needs to be wooed.

Whatever the final choice made by the Champenois, one thing

is clear: there will be no serious problem until after the year 2000. The stocks held in Champagne can easily meet the expected demand. The region has a breathing space. In the sheer quality of its very finest wines, Champagne is untouchable. With all its new developments and a dedication to raising quality through improved viticulture, control of yields, winemaking and, very importantly, ageing, if it can lift the quality at all price levels, then it will remain unbeatable. But if, for purely commercial reasons, it should not continue on this path but return to the over-production of the young, green wines of the 1980s, then it will almost certainly meet with a strong challenge from overseas – except for the very finest Champagne wines, which will certainly remain outstanding and command the premium they so richly deserve.

APPENDIX I

Les Grandes Dames

─────

SIR FRANCIS: Hang't, if I am baulked both in love and
revenge, the cross adventures shall be drowned in brisk
champagne.
'Tis the dear glass which eases every smart,
And presently does cure the aching heart.
from *The Innocent Mistress*, Act IV Sc. II, by Mary Pix,
first performed c. June 1697

No book on champagne would be complete without reference to
the lives and work of the great ladies of the region who have had
an enormous effect on the wine, whether by being involved in its
development or its commercial side. Each of these ladies was a
'Champagne widow' whose influence began only on the death of
her husband.

First came the Veuve Clicquot, who, as we have seen, inspired the
development of *remuage*. Nicole-Barbe Ponsardin married François
Clicquot at the end of the eighteenth century. As all the churches
were closed following the 1789 Revolution, the wedding took
place in a wine cellar, a splendid and most appropriate venue
foreshadowing the future. Widowed aged only twenty-seven, this
remarkable woman persuaded her father-in-law to let her run the
business, which she did very successfully until her death in 1866
aged eighty-eight. Undoubtedly, part of her success was due to her
percipient choice of associates, but that should not detract from
her drive and energy in what was then an entirely male preserve.
Despite the Napoleonic Wars, with the help of her able salesman,
Heinrich Bohne, she so dominated the Russian market that others
retired hurt, and not until the champagnes of Louis Roederer
also arrived in Moscow and St Petersburg was there any serious

competition. In 1828, when the Paris bank which handled the Clicquot finances collapsed, she was saved by the actions of her well-chosen man of business, Edouard Werlé, who used his private fortune to pay off the creditors. In gratitude, Mme Clicquot made M. Werlé a partner and very wisely left the business to him, rather than to her daughter, Clémentine, who had married the charming, extravagant, but penniless Comte Louis de Chevigné.

Jeanne Alexandrine Louise Pommery, so far as is known, had taken no interest in the business until her husband died in 1858, leaving her with two children, one of whom, Louise, was still a baby. Two years previously M. Pommery had invested in the firm of N. Greno & Cie to such an extent that on his death his widow succeeded and took control. M. Greno remained with the firm for a short while and advised the inexperienced widow well.

The then Pommery house was occupied by the Prussian Governor of Reims during the 1870–71 Franco-Prussian war, and after their withdrawal Mme Pommery developed the business, first by enlarging her cellars. She appears to have been one of the first to realise the potential importance of the chalk pits, or *crayères*, for storage and ageing, and purchased 60 hectares of land for that purpose. Then she foresaw the necessity of owning vineyards and bought 300 hectares in fine sites. The extraordinary buildings in Parc Pommery were also her brainchild, took eight years to build, and lie above the amazing cellars. She died in 1890.

Three years previously, Eugène Laurent, the husband of Mathilde Perrier, died. His widow immediately took over the reins of the family business, Veuve Laurent-Perrier, and controlled it for just under forty years, selling over half a million bottles per annum before the outbreak of the First World War. When Mathilde died childless in 1925 the house was finally acquired by the widow Marie-Louise de Nonancourt, née Lanson in 1938.

What Mesdames Clicquot, Laurent and Pommery did for their houses in the nineteenth century was repeated for the firm of Louis Roederer this century by Camille Olry-Roederer, widow of the great-nephew of the founder. She ran the company for some forty-two years after her husband's death in 1932, when the company had not yet recovered from the (to them) disastrous 1917 Russian Revolution, when overnight 80 per cent of their market disappeared, added to which the new government declined to pay the outstanding bills of the previous regime. Mme Olry-Roederer had one advantage over the earlier widows: she had acted as her husband's assistant. Like Mme Pommery, she realised that investment in vineyards would be important, and so built the company's holdings that today about 80 per cent of the grapes needed come from their own vines. A tremendously stylish lady, she always dressed finely and wore much jewellery, and was rightly regarded as a magnificent ambassadress for Champagne.

The legendary, and lovingly remembered, Mme Jacques Bollinger, known as Tante Lily to the family and as Lily Bollinger to the rest of the world, took over the firm of Bollinger following the death of her husband, in 1941, at an enormously difficult time. Jacques Bollinger had been a highly decorated airman during the First World War, but his health was never strong and he died, aged forty-seven, leaving his widow to run the company. It was an acutely critical time for Champagne, but Mme Jacques, as her estate workers knew her, was childless and a tirelessly hard worker. She would cycle regularly through the vineyards every day, often before arriving at her desk. Despite the obvious difficulties, she would fill in all the paperwork required by the occupying German forces, negotiate for the best possible fertilisers, insist on the highest standards in making the wine and, as bombing raids grew with the approaching liberation, would be found helping the wounded or rehousing the homeless. After the war, as new and modern methods came to Champagne, Mme Jacques was always concerned first and foremost with quality, and took a very conservative position, insisting on honouring tradition. Not for her the *blanc de blancs* and lighter styles. Champagne, she would say, is a blended wine. She is justly famous for the words, 'I drink [champagne] when I am happy and when I am sad. Sometimes I drink it when I'm alone. When I have company I consider it obligatory. I trifle with it if I'm not hungry and drink it when I am. Otherwise I never touch it – unless I'm thirsty.' Mme Bollinger died in 1977, leaving a house famous for its quality.

Today, there is a new and very energetic widow at the head of a large Champagne house. Carol Duval is of Belgian parentage. She married Jean-Charles Duval of Duval Leroy, and became involved with the business by initially taking charge of the harvest. On her husband's sudden death in 1991, Mme Duval could have sold up, but instead became President of the company and has poured her energies into modernising the plant and opening up export markets. Previously, most of the Duval Leroy wines were sold under different labels, but Mme Duval is determined to change this and build up the name of the brand. Undoubtedly, another great Champagne Widow, but this time in the making.

APPENDIX 2

The Wine Orders

Sometimes referred to as 'heralds' for a wine-producing region, Champagne, like other areas, has its Ordres and Confréries. In fact, it has no less than seven of them, the last being founded as late as 27 June 1997.

L'ORDRE DES COTEAUX DE LA CHAMPAGNE

First named in the seventeenth century, and originally a title given in mockery, this is the oldest association. Two of the group of noblemen who were its first members, the Marquis de Sillery and the Marquis de St Evremond, were prime movers in spreading the knowledge of champagne wines. Having served Champagne well, the order as such died out.

It was restarted in 1956 by François Taittinger and René Gaucher as an ambassador for the region's wines. Today, it has a worldwide membership, united by their love and admiration for Champagne. It holds Chapitres at which new members are admitted, and has begun to offer members special seminars in Champagne. It has been so successful that in 1999 the Ordre moves to purpose-built premises in Cuisles which are intended to become a promotional centre.

39 rue de Talleyrand, 51100 Reims

COMMANDERIE DU SAULTE-BOUCHON CHAMPENOIS

This order was founded in 1975 by growers in the Aube to promote the Aubois champagnes. Its name is taken from an old nickname, given in the seventeenth century, for the then new sparkling wines; translated it means 'jumping-cork wine'. On the order's seal are featured the arms of Thibault IV, Count of Champagne, and their patron saint, Bernard of Clairvaux, locally believed to be the father of the Aube vineyards.

Hôtel de Ville de Troyes, 63 boulevard Blanqui, 10000 Troyes

CONFRÉRIE DES ECHEVINS DE BOUZY

The public perception of Bouzy is first and foremost as a producer of red wines – Bouzy Rouge – but it does produce both white and *rosé* champagnes. In 1979 the Confrérie was created to promote all the different wines of Bouzy and their distinctive styles.

Mairie de Bouzy, 51150 Bouzy

CONFRÉRIE DES VIGNERONS DE SÉZANNE

With the replanting of the Sézanne vineyards to their full extent over the last twenty years, the Confrérie was founded to honour this and to promote the area and its wines. It is involved in all the activities of the growers, including wine fairs and grape-harvest dinners, and has organised a Quality Charter for its members.

9 rue d'Epernay, 51120 Sézanne

ORDRE DU TABLIER BLANC

This order was founded recently by Jacques Vazart, a grower in Chouilly, to promote the image of the white apron. This apron was originally worn by highly skilled cellar workers in Champagne during the nineteenth and early twentieth centuries, namely the *remueurs*. The intention of the Ordre is to remind people of the quality and prestige associated with the wearing of the white apron.

c/o M. Vazart, 6 rue des Partelaines, 51200 Chouilly

CONFRÉRIE DU PINOT MEUNIER

This is a recent order, founded in September 1995, which supports and promotes the champagnes of this area, which are mainly made from Pinot Meunier. It also organises the Fair of the Wines.

Place du Général de Gaulle, 02310 Mairie de Charly-sur-Marne

COMMANDERIE DU CHARDONNAY

Only just founded in Villers-Marméry, the objective of this group is to promote Chardonnay and the wines made from it.

Bollinger Charter of Ethics and Quality

PREAMBLE

Each French Wine Appellation defines:

1. A geographic origin, viticultural practices and a method of vinification which is adhered to by all those that carry that Appellation,
2. Quality references that are recognised by the consumer.

Each Appellation produces a wide variety of wines that have different standards of quality. The *échelle des crus* – i.e. the rating scale within each Appellation – accurately defines levels of quality and offers references that consumers recognise and understand. The highest echelon sets quality references and establishes the image for the area.

In Champagne, however, the *échelle des crus* is not known to the consumer and therefore he does not have those references which would guide him in his understanding of the area and of the differences in quality of the wines of Champagne.

Morever, at a time when sparkling wines – some offering high standards of quality – are being produced in many parts of the world, it is essential that a Grand Vin de Champagne reiterates its difference and its prime position. For these reasons, Bollinger finds it necessary to promulgate this Charter and set forth:

1. the principles of *Ethics* which govern the usage of the Bollinger name;
2. the rules of *Quality* that Bollinger is committed to following,

and, therefore, give consumers the quality references they require for a better understanding of Bollinger's distinctive style and the quality of its wines.

By promulgating such a charter, it is not Bollinger's intent to claim, or dictate, the only set of rules that should govern quality in a *Grand Vin de Champagne*, or to be so pretentious as to give anyone lessons.

This Charter is a definitive commitment, a fundamental pledge by the House of Bollinger to remain faithful, ethically and qualitatively, to the basic tenets, in its view, of a *Grand Vin de Champagne*.

ETHICS

The rules of authenticity which govern the usage of the Bollinger name:

1. The House of Bollinger uses the name Bollinger to qualify solely a *Vin de Champagne*. Thus, it excludes the use of the name Bollinger for all other sparkling wines.
2. The name Bollinger defines wines which are vinified – from the pressing of the grapes – by the House of Bollinger. In extremely rare cases, a small amount of *vins clairs** are purchased and added to the rest.

QUALITY

The means which express the excellence of the Champagne Appellation.

The Charter of Quality deals with five primary areas:

- origin of the musts
- first fermentation
- importance of the pH
- maturation on the lees

In these different fields, the House of Bollinger continually studies, researches and tastes, in order to adapt itself if necessary to the evolution of technology and oenology.

* wine after racking and before bottling for second fermentation

1. Grapes

1.1 Bollinger's Vineyards

Bollinger's vineyards consist of 144 hectares. These supply 70 per cent of its grape requirements.

By controlling such a large percentage of its supply of grapes, Bollinger ensures the continuity of the style of its wines.

The House of Bollinger has selected for its Pinot Noir vineyards the Pinot *Moret* (clone 386) and is currently studying other clones (521 & 743, for instance).

A number of research studies made by official institutions show that this clone, 386, ensures the typicity of the terroir and maintains reasonable yields. The House of Bollinger endeavours to develop the terroir typicity in each and every one of its vineyards.

1.2 Harvest
In years when grapes are affected by rot, and when conditions allow, hand-sorting and selection of bunches take place.

1.3 Blend
The vast majority of the grapes Bollinger uses come from *grand* and *premier cru* vineyards. Bollinger is committed to:

– a minimum of 95 per cent for the Vintages
– a minimum of 80 per cent for the Special Cuvée

The use of grands crus and premiers crus ensures the continuity and consistency of Bollinger's distinctive style and quality of wine: vinosity, elegance, complexity and depth.

Bollinger blends are made exclusively from 30 different *crus* from the Departement of the Marne, of which 10 are *grands crus* and 14 *premiers crus*.

This secures the balance and quality of Bollinger wines.

The blends are constituted, on average, of:

	Vintages	
	Grande Année and RD	Special Cuvée
Pinot Noir	62% (35% from Aÿ)	60% (35% from Aÿ)
Chardonnay	35%	25%
Pinot Meunier	3% (0% in most vintages)	15%

The backbone of the Bollinger blends, therefore of the Bollinger style, is the Pinot Noir from grand cru *vineyards, which gives the wine its vinosity and complexity; the Chardonnay adds elegance and finesse; Pinot Meunier imparts freshness and lightness.*

2. The Wines

2.1 Bollinger only uses the *cuvées*

After pressing, the House of Bollinger keeps the *cuvées* – i.e. the first pressings – and sells off its first and second *tailles* – i.e. the second and third pressings. If, however, the harvest is excellent, the House of Bollinger will keep the first *tailles* of Chardonnay. Bollinger wines, Special Cuvée and Vintages are made exclusively, or almost exclusively, from wines of the *cuvée*.

At harvest, the average pH of the cuvée *fluctuates between 2.9 and 3, while that of the first* tailles *fluctuates between 3.1 and 3.15 (the first* tailles *of Chardonnay have a lower pH than that of the Pinots), and that of the second* tailles *between 3.2 and 3.3. The* cuvées *have the lowest pH, and the lower the pH, the less the wine will be subject to bacterial influences and oxidation, and the better the wine will keep and mature.*

2.2 The first fermentation of Vintage and Reserve wines takes place in casks

First fermentation of Vintage and Reserve wines takes place in 200- or 400-litre oak casks.

The quality of the must – cuvée *of grands crus* and *premiers crus – allows Bollinger to ferment* les grandes années *in casks. Barrel fermentation has a different effect on wines from fermentation in stainless steel tanks. Barrels create a gentle oxidation and the contact with the wood gives the wine a specific style which can only be achieved with musts of sound quality: the* cuvées *of grands* and *premiers crus. Wines fermented in cask have a lower pH and therefore are better preserved. The small volume of the cask allows a natural and rapid fining of the wines. Each* cru *can be closely and individually followed, lot by lot. The pH of the Vintage wines fluctuates between 2.9 and 3.02.*

2.3 The first fermentation of the base wines for the Special Cuvée takes place in tanks

Wines of the year that are destined to be used for the Special Cuvée blend are fermented in stainless steel tanks.

In average or poor years, when grapes are not fully ripe and are excessively acid, to obtain a perfectly sound wine, Bollinger needs to control the malolactic fermentation as much as possible, a control which is easier to achieve in tanks.

The wine obtained is therefore sound and constitutes the base for the Special Cuvée, to which 5 to 10 per cent Reserve wines will be added to perfect the blend. The pH of the Special Cuvée fluctuates between 3 and 3.05.

2.4 Reserve wines aged in Magnums
In order to maintain the continuity of quality and style demanded by Bollinger for its Special Cuvée, it is blended with between 5 and 10 per cent Reserve wines. These Reserve wines come from *grand cru* and *premier cru* vineyards and, having had a slight second fermentation, are kept in magnum, *cru* by *cru*, Vintage by Vintage.

In this way, they avoid premature oxidation since the slight prise de mousse – *i.e. the second fermentation – protects the wine in a reductive state. The Magnum size gives an ideal balance between air and wine for long keeping.*

2.5 Three years' minimum ageing prior to disgorgement
A *Grand Vin de Champagne* needs time to develop its personality, its great complexity, its various flavours. Long ageing on the lees allows Bollinger wines to develop these characteristics, which are the basis of the Bollinger style and quality.

Bollinger Special Cuvée	3 years of age minimum
Bollinger Grande Année	5 years of age minimum
Bollinger RD	8 years of age minimum

All Vintage wines are *sous bouchage liège*.

Once the wine has been bottled and has undergone second fermentation, it goes from an oxidative* state to a reductive† state: it is protected from oxygen by its cork and rests in contact with

* state with oxygen
† state without oxygen

the carbonic gas resulting from the second fermentation. Its redox potential is therefore greatly lowered.

This low redox potential promotes the development of the aromas and flavours because the wine can age safely over a period of several years only if it undergoes as slow an oxidation as possible.

After two or three years in bottle, the oxidation of a wine sous liège* and sous capsule† are virtually identical. However, after five or six years the two wines start to show differences. The measure of the redox potential shows that the wine sous liège has experienced markedly less oxidation. As previously mentioned, flavours and aromas develop when the wine is in a reductive state. It is therefore essential to use bouchage liège *if one wants to age a wine a long enough time for it to develop its full flavour potential.*

The action of the yeasts during maturation time is vital. First, they activate the prise de mousse; *second, the yeast autolysis frees the aroma precursors which contribute to the formation of flavours. RD is a perfect example of the above.*

2.6 Three months' minimum rest after disgorgement
After disgorging, Bollinger wines stay in the cellars for a minimum of three months before shipping.

This final rest allows the wine to settle after the shock of disgorgement, to assimilate its liqueur de dosage, *and to recover a balance suitable for tasting.*

* under real cork
† under crown cork

APPENDIX 4

Members of the Union of Wine Producers

━━━━━

L'UNION des MAISONS de CHAMPAGNE
1 rue Marie-Stuart, BP 2185
51081 Reims
tel: 03 26 47 26 89
fax: 03 26 47 48 44

ABELÉ
52 rue de Sillery, BP 18
51051 Reims
tel: 03 26 87 79 80
fax: 03 26 87 79 81

ALAIN THIÉNOT
14 rue des Moissons
51100 Reims
tel: 03 26 77 50 10
fax: 03 26 77 50 19

ARNOULT Jean
100 Grand Rue, BP 7
10110 Celles-sur-Ource
tel: 03 25 38 50 06
fax: 03 25 38 58 01

AYALA
2 bld du Nord, BP 6
51160 Aÿ
tel: 03 26 55 15 44
fax: 03 26 51 09 04

BEAUMET
3 rue Malakoff, BP 247
51207 Epernay

tel: 03 26 59 50 10
fax: 03 26 54 78 52

BESSERAT de BELLEFON
19 avenue de Champagne, BP 36
51202 Epernay
tel: 03 26 78 50 50
fax: 03 26 36 39 09

BILLECART-SALMON
40 rue Carnot
51530 Mareuil-sur-Aÿ
tel: 03 26 52 60 22
fax: 03 26 52 64 88

BOIZEL
16 rue de Bernon, BP 149
51205 Epernay
tel: 03 26 55 21 51
fax: 03 26 54 31 83

BOLLINGER
16 rue Jules Lobet, BP 4
51160 Aÿ
tel: 03 26 53 33 66
fax: 03 26 54 85 59

F. BONNET Père et Fils
Rue du Mesnil, Oger
51190 Avize
tel: 03 26 57 52 43
fax: 03 26 57 78 65

BOULARD Raymond
La Neuville-aux-Larris
51480 Damery
tel: 03 26 58 12 08
fax: 03 26 58 13 02

BRICE
3 rue Yvonnet
51150 Bouzy
tel: 03 26 52 06 60
fax: 03 26 57 05 07

A. BROUCAT & KOCH
29 rempart du Midi
51190 Avize
tel: 03 26 53 30 00
fax: 03 26 57 59 26

Edouard BRUN & Cie
14 rue Marcel Mailly, BP 11
51160 Aÿ
tel: 03 26 55 20 11
fax: 03 26 51 94 29

BRUNO PAILLARD
Avenue de Champagne
51100 Reims
tel: 03 26 36 20 22
fax: 03 26 36 57 72

CANARD-DUCHÊNE
1 rue Edmond Canard, Ludes
51500 Rilly-la-Montagne
tel: 03 26 61 10 96
fax: 03 26 61 13 90

CATTIER
6 et 11 rue Dom Pérignon, BP 15
51500 Chigny-les-Roses
tel: 03 26 03 42 11
fax: 03 26 03 43 13

CHAMPAVIZE
26 rue Pasteur, BP 13
51190 Avize
tel: 03 26 57 54 98
fax: 03 26 57 55 20

CHANOINE Frères
Avenue de Champagne
51100 Reims
tel: 03 26 36 61 60
fax: 03 26 36 66 62

A. CHAUVET & SARL CHAUVET
41 avenue de Champagne, BP 4
51150 Tours-sur-Marne
tel: 03 26 58 92 37
fax: 03 26 58 96 31

DE CASTELLANE
57 rue de Verdun, BP 136
51204 Epernay
tel: 03 26 51 19 19
fax: 03 26 54 24 81

DE CAZANOVE
1 rue des Côtelles, BP 118
51204 Epernay
tel: 03 26 59 57 40
fax: 03 26 54 16 38

DELAHAIE
18 rue Porte Lucas
51200 Epernay
tel: 03 26 54 08 74
fax: 03 26 54 34 45

DELBECK
39 rue du Général Sarrail
51100 Reims
tel: 03 26 77 58 00
fax: 03 26 77 58 01

DEMOISELLE
42 avenue de Champagne
51200 Epernay
tel: 03 26 53 33 20
fax: 03 26 51 87 07

SA DEREGARD MASSING
BP 20
51190 Avize
tel: 03 26 57 52 92
fax: 03 26 57 78 23

A. DESMOULINS
44 avenue Foch, BP 10
51201 Epernay
tel: 03 26 54 24 24
fax: 03 26 54 26 15

DE TELMONT
1 avenue de Champagne, BP 17
51480 Damery
tel: 03 26 58 40 33
fax: 03 26 58 63 93

DEUTZ
16 rue Jeanson, BP 9
51160 Aÿ
tel: 03 26 55 15 11
fax: 03 26 54 01 21

DE VENOGE & Cie
30 avenue de Champagne, BP 103
51204 Epernay
tel: 03 26 53 34 34
fax: 03 26 53 34 35

DILIGENT François
Buxeuil
10110 Bar-sur-Seine
tel: 03 25 38 50 76
fax: 03 25 38 57 72

DUVAL LEROY
69 avenue Bammental, BP 37
51130 Vertus
tel: 03 26 52 10 75
fax: 03 26 52 12 93

GARDET & Co
13 rue C. Legros
51500 Chigny-les-Roses
tel: 03 26 03 42 03
fax: 03 26 03 43 95

GEORGE GOULET
1 avenue de Paris, BP 2045
51072 Reims
tel: 03 26 66 44 88
fax: 03 26 67 99 36

H. GERMAIN & Fils
38 rue de Reims, BP 1
51500 Rilly-la-Montagne
tel: 03 26 03 40 19
fax: 03 26 03 43 11

Paul GOBILLARD
Château de Pierry
51200 Epernay
tel: 03 26 54 05 11
fax: 03 26 54 46 03

GOSSET
69 rue Jules Blondeau, BP 7
51160 Aÿ
tel: 03 26 56 99 56
fax: 03 26 51 55 88

GRATIEN MEYER SEYDOUX
30 rue M. Cerveaux, BP 3
51201 Epernay
tel: 03 26 54 38 20
fax: 03 26 54 53 44

HAMM & fils
16 rue N. Philipponat, BP 27
51160 Aÿ
tel: 03 26 55 44 19
fax: 03 26 51 98 68

HEIDSIECK & Co MONOPOLE
17 avenue de Champagne, BP 150
51205 Epernay
tel: 03 26 59 50 50
fax: 03 26 52 19 65

Charles HEIDSIECK
4 bld Henry Vasnier, BP 129
51055 Reims
tel: 03 26 84 43 50
fax: 03 26 84 43 86

HENRIOT
3 place des Droits de l'Homme
51100 Reims
tel: 03 26 89 53 00
fax: 03 26 89 53 10

HÉRARD ET FLUTEAU
5 rue de la Nation
10250 Gye-sur-Seine
tel: 03 25 38 20 02
fax: 03 25 38 24 84

IRROY
42 boulevard Lundy
51100 Reims
tel: 03 26 85 45 35
fax: 03 26 85 44 39

IVERNEL
4 rue Jules Lobet, BP 15
51160 Aÿ
tel: 03 26 55 21 10
fax: 03 26 51 55 88

JACQUESSON & Fils
68 rue du Cl Fabien
51530 Dizy
tel: 03 26 55 68 11
fax: 03 26 51 06 25

JACQUINOT
34 rue M. Cerveaux, BP 48
51202 Epernay
tel: 03 26 54 36 81
fax: 03 26 55 67 33

JAMART & Cie
BP 1
51200 St-Martin-d'Ablois
tel: 03 26 59 92 78
fax: 03 26 59 95 23

JEANMAIRE
12 rue Godart Roger, BP 256
51207 Epernay
tel: 03 26 59 50 10
fax: 03 26 54 78 52

JOSEPH PERRIER
69 avenue de Paris, BP 31
51005 Châlons-en-Champagne
tel: 03 26 68 29 51
fax: 03 26 70 57 16

KRUG
5 rue Coquebert, BP 22
51051 Reims
tel: 03 26 84 44 20
fax: 03 26 84 44 49

Charles **LAFITTE**
39 rue du Général Leclerc
51130 Vertus
tel: 03 26 59 50 50
fax: 03 26 52 19 65

René-James **LALLIER SA**
4 place de la Libération, BP 5
51160 Aÿ
tel: 03 26 55 43 40
fax: 03 26 58 25 18

LANSON P & F/MASSÉ
12 bld Lundy, BP 163
51056 Reims
tel: 03 26 78 50 50
fax: 03 26 78 53 88

Pierre **LAURAIN**
2 rue Roger Sondag, BP 46
51160 Aÿ
tel: 03 26 55 18 90
fax: 03 26 55 19 34

Veuve **LAURENT-PERRIER**
Avenue de Champagne, BP 3
51150 Tours-sur-Marne
tel: 03 26 58 91 22
fax: 03 26 58 95 10

Albert **LE BRUN** (SCEV)
93 avenue de Paris, BP 204
51009 Châlons-en-Champagne
tel: 03 26 68 18 68
fax: 03 26 21 53 31

LEMOINE
66 rue de Chigny, BP 3
51500 Rilly-la-Montagne
tel: 03 26 03 40 25
fax: 03 26 03 42 88

LENOBLE
BP 6
51480 Damery
tel: 03 26 58 42 60
fax: 03 26 58 65 57

MANSARD BAILLET
14 rue Chaude Ruelle, BP 187
51206 Epernay
tel: 03 26 54 18 55
fax: 03 26 51 99 50

MARIE STUART
8 pl de la République, BP 268
51069 Reims
tel: 03 26 77 50 50
fax: 03 26 77 50 59

MARNE & CHAMPAGNE
22 rue M. Cerveaux, BP 138
51205 Epernay
tel: 03 26 78 50 50
fax: 03 26 54 55 77

Sté VINICOLE MARTIN & Fils
3 rue Aristide Briand, BP 3
51150 Bouzy
tel: 03 26 51 87 76
fax: 03 26 51 87 89

G. H. MARTEL et Cie
69 avenue de Champagne, BP
  1011
51318 Epernay
tel: 03 26 51 06 33
fax: 03 26 54 41 52

MÉDOT & Cie
19 route de Dormans
51390 Pargny-lès-Reims

tel: 03 26 49 20 09
fax: 03 26 49 24 93

MERCIER
20 avenue de Champagne, BP 134
51204 Epernay
tel: 03 26 54 71 11
fax: 03 26 54 84 23

MOËT ET CHANDON
20 avenue de Champagne, BP 140
51333 Epernay
tel: 03 26 51 20 00
fax: 03 26 54 84 23

MONGARDIEN-SOUTIRAN
12 rue Saint-Vincent, BP 12
51150 Ambonnay
tel: 03 26 57 07 87
fax: 03 26 57 81 74

MONTAUDON
6 rue Ponsardin, BP 2742
51061 Reims
tel: 03 26 47 53 30
fax: 03 26 47 88 82

MONTEBELLO
2 bld du Nord
51160 Aÿ
tel: 03 26 55 15 44
fax: 03 26 51 09 04

Jean MOUTARDIER
Le Breuil
51210 Montmirail
tel: 03 26 59 21 09
fax: 03 26 59 21 25

G. H. MUMM & Cie
29 rue du champ de Mars
BP 2712, 51053 Reims
tel: 03 26 49 59 69
fax: 03 26 40 46 13

PERRIER-JOUET
28 avenue de Champagne, BP 31
51201 Epernay
tel: 03 26 53 38 00
fax: 03 26 54 54 55

PHILIPPONNAT/LEPITRE
13 rue du Pont, BP 2
51160 Mareuil-sur-Aÿ
tel: 03 26 56 93 00
fax: 03 26 56 93 18

Jules PIERLOT
15 rue Henri Martin, BP 219
51207 Epernay
tel: 03 26 54 45 52
fax: 03 26 55 55 18

PIPER HEIDSIECK
51 bld Henry Vasnier, BP 106
51054 Reims
tel: 03 26 84 43 00
fax: 03 26 84 43 49

PLOYEZ JACQUEMART
Ludes
51500 Rilly-la-Montagne
tel: 03 26 61 11 87
fax: 03 26 61 12 20

POL ROGER
3 rue Henri Lelarge, BP 199
51206 Epernay
tel: 03 26 59 58 00
fax: 03 26 55 25 70

POMMERY SA
5 pl. du Général Gouraud, BP 87
51053 Reims
tel: 03 26 61 62 63
fax: 03 26 61 62 99

C. H. & A. PRIEUR
2 rue Villers-au-Bois, BP 41
51130 Vertus
tel: 03 26 52 11 74
fax: 03 26 52 29 10

PRIN Père & Fils
24 chemin de la Grange aux Bois
51530 Chavot-Courcourt
tel: 03 26 54 32 74
fax: 03 26 07 77 71

Eugène RALLE
BP 6
51360 Verzenay
tel: 03 26 49 40 12
fax: 03 26 49 44 40

G. RÉMY
15 rue de Longchamps, BP 44
Cerseuil-en-Champagne
51700 Dormans
tel: 03 26 58 28 94
fax: 03 26 58 88 10

Louis ROEDERER
21 bld Lundy, BP 66
51053 Reims
tel: 03 26 40 42 11
fax: 03 26 47 66 51

Théophile ROEDERER
21 bld Lundy, BP 1214
51058 Reims
tel: 03 26 40 19 00
fax: 03 26 84 92 37

RUINART (SRGV)
4 rue des Crayères
51053 Reims
tel: 03 26 77 51 51
fax: 03 26 82 88 43

LOUIS DE SACY
6 rue de Verzenay, BP 2
51380 Verzy
tel: 03 26 97 91 13
fax: 03 26 97 94 25

SALON & DELAMOTTE
Société AS
5 rue de la Brêche, BP 3
51190 Le Mesnil-sur-Oger

tel: 03 26 57 51 65
fax: 03 26 57 79 29

SENEZ Cristian
Fontette
10360 Essoyes
tel: 03 25 29 60 62
fax: 03 25 29 64 63

TAITTINGER
9 place Saint-Nicaise, BP 2741
51061 Reims
tel: 03 26 85 45 45
fax: 03 26 85 44 46

TROUILLARD
2 avenue Foch, BP 272
51208 Epernay
tel: 03 26 55 37 55
fax: 03 26 55 46 36

Veuve CLICQUOT PONSARDIN
12 rue du Temple, BP 102
51054 Reims
tel: 03 26 89 54 40
fax: 03 26 40 60 17

VRANKEN
BP 3, Bouzy
51150 Tours-sur-Marne
tel: 03 26 59 50 50
fax: 03 26 52 19 65

APPENDIX 5
Vintages

═══════

1945 As if to celebrate the end of the Second World War, a small if very elegant vintage which lasted extremely well.

1946 A year for NV styles. Not declared as a vintage.

1947 A vintage year for most houses which produced long-lived but very fruity wines.

1948 A fairly large harvest giving good-quality NV wines, but very little vintage.

1949 A very good quality harvest yielding elegant wines with excellent fruit and powerful acidity, leading to a long life.

1950 A large harvest, mainly giving NV styles. Little vintage was made.

1951 Rather thin, acidic wines from a small yield and no vintage made.

1952 Fine, well-balanced wines from a year when most houses declared a vintage. The occasional bottles found at auction can be well worth the money.

1953 The second fine vintage in a row, very well balanced and full of fruit.

1954 A relatively large harvest, mainly used in the production of NV wines of considerable style and elegance.

1955 A large harvest which was widely declared as a vintage, although underrated at the time. The wines showed excellent acidity and elegant fruit.

1956 Average quality wines only from what was an above-average-size harvest. No vintage declarations.

1957 A very small yield following savage spring frosts. Of ordinary quality. No vintage wine.

1958 An average-sized crop of fairly ordinary wines. No vintages declared.

1959 An exceptional vintage, following a number of poor years, making very rich, full-bodied wines. Unanimously declared a vintage.

1960 Good average wines, not of vintage quality, but making very decent NV styles.

1961 A difficult start to the year was followed by good ripening conditions. Widely declared as a vintage, the wines were rich, with supporting acidity, albeit from a small crop.

1962 Another low-yielding harvest, which developed in cool conditions and was saved by a good warm September leading to fruity and supple wines of vintage quality.

1963 Very poor weather conditions led to an average-sized harvest of wines only suitable for NV blends.

1964 A very high quality year which, after a hot and dry growing season, produced very big, long-lived, fruity wines, some of which can still be found. The best vintage wines benefited tremendously from long bottle ageing.

1965 A very difficult year where bad weather led not only to *coulure* and *millerandage*, but later on to serious attacks of rot. NV styles only.

1966 Despite serious winter frosts and hail damage during the growing season, and some mildew, this harvest was saved by good weather at picking and was generally declared a vintage, producing elegant and well-balanced wines.

1967 A near-disastrous year for weather, with widespread winter frost killing a large number of vines and grey rot further reducing yields. Mostly NV wines.

1968 Disastrous weather conditions, beginning with heavy spring frosts, to be followed later by hail and then rot, led to a small harvest of rather thin wines used almost totally for blending.

1969 Fluctuating temperatures and heavy rain led to considerable *coulure* and serious outbreaks of mildew. But good, dry conditions during the harvest enabled vintage wines to be made, albeit with higher than usual acidity.

1970 After a cold, damp spring, growing conditions were excellent leading to what, at the time, was the largest recorded harvest. Most houses declared a vintage of rich wines with excellent acidity.

1971 Uneven weather conditions, including violent storms in late July and massive hail on 18 August, were followed by a dry and hot September leading to a small harvest giving very stylish wines of great finesse, some of which have lasted remarkably well.

1972 A wet year, following some serious frosts, further damaged by early frosts before the harvest, produced very average wines. No vintage wines were made.

1973 Excellent growing conditions during the summer were followed by heavy rain during September leading to considerable rot in the vineyards. However, some very agreeable, if light, vintage wines were produced showing strong acidity, but with an attractive aroma.

1974 A year of very difficult weather conditions with rain setting in just before the vintage. The wines were of very variable quality, with those from the earliest picked grapes being the best.

1975 A wet winter was followed by snow in March leading to a late bud break. Hot, but not necessarily sunny, weather led to a lateish harvest of healthy grapes giving well-balanced wines with excellent fruit and a good level of acidity.

1976 After a very dry winter, this was the year of the great drought and unusual heat, which in turn led to the harvest starting very early on 1 September. A large harvest yielding wines of great richness and extract, but relatively low in acidity. Despite this, many of the wines have lasted well although their sheer power makes them atypical.

1977 A very poor summer following the volcanic eruption on Mount St Helens (the dust from which, driven by the prevailing winds, formed a screen in the atmosphere blocking much of the sun's strength). This led to a late harvest of rather light wines. Not a vintage year.

1978 A very small crop following a poor and very late flowering and heavily affected by rot. Although a couple of houses did declare a vintage, the wines are not typical and often lack structure.

1979 After an exceptionally cold winter and frosts in early May, the weather turned warm and sunny, giving a large harvest of very healthy grapes. In spite of rain during the *vendange*, sugar levels were excellent and acidity strong, producing firm, fruity and stylish wines which have lasted well.

1980 A late and small harvest after a summer cooler than usual, saved only by a sunny September. The wines were aromatic and fresh, but rather acidic in general. One or two houses managed to make some vintage wines, but mostly a year for NV blending.

1981 Generally a wet year, but an unusually warm March produced forward vine development which was then cut back by April frosts and hail in May. *Coulure* at flowering also reduced the potential crop, leading to a small harvest at a time when stocks in the cellars were low. The wines were mostly used for blending, but a small amount of elegant vintage wines was produced.

1982 A large crop of very healthy grapes was produced following almost perfect growing conditions, spoilt only by rain after the first week of the harvest. Classic, elegant wines, widely declared as a vintage, and which have lasted and developed well with bottle age.

1983 A second year with a large crop of high-quality, healthy grapes, following almost ideal growing conditions. Rich wines with a high malic acid content, they are well balanced and potentially very long-lived.

1984 A cold, wet spring with fluctuating temperatures at flowering leading to considerable *coulure* and a much reduced crop resulted in a late harvest exacerbated by low sunshine during September. Not a vintage year.

1985 The severe winter with temperatures going as low as 25°C. destroyed about 10 per cent of the vines. This was followed by damp and dull conditions which continued until July. A very sunny, early autumn changed the picture completely, and this harvest, although small, produced very stylish wines with an amazing balance between fruit, acidity and alcohol. Almost every house declared a vintage and the best wines continue to improve.

1986 Yet again the spring weather was poor, but the summer was warm and sunny until August and early September when rain intervened. Some good wines were declared by those who selected the grapes carefully as rot was a problem.

1987 On the whole, poor weather throughout a damp summer made grey rot a problem. However, fine weather later in the year and during the harvest meant that a large crop of useful NV blending wines could be picked.

1988 The first of three very good years, although the quantity was slightly reduced. A spring without frost, and good flowering in almost perfect conditions, boded well, but a cooler cloudy July, followed by heavy rain as the vintage approached, led to careful selection and less quantity than in 1987. Powerful, fruity, well-structured vintage wines were produced.

1989 An early spring, spoilt only by some late frosts, was followed by virtually ideal growing conditions. Flowering was early and a hot summer with plenty of sunshine led to very ripe healthy grapes. Very high quality, appealing vintage wines – drinking well now, but with plenty of life remaining in them.

1990 Despite some frost damage in April, there was a good flowering, although *coulure* did occur. A hot, dry summer resulted in a second crop which helped to rectify the loss created by the early frosts. Alcohol and acidity levels were excellent and most houses have declared a 1990 vintage.

1991 Spring frosts in April and May caused concern, but as the weather improved replacement buds were formed. From the end of June onwards a hot summer helped the grapes to develop, but about ten days before the harvest the weather broke causing dilution. Not truly a vintage year, although one or two makers did manage to produce light but elegant wines. Mostly, however, a year for NV.

1992 Potentially a large harvest of healthy grapes, but a benchmark year. Following the market problems, new measures to limit both the size of the crop and the amount of juice extracted came into being. This resulted in the very sad sight of unwanted bunches of grapes being allowed to rot on the vine or lying cut in the vineyards. Again, some growers managed to produce vintage wines, but in general it was not declared.

1993 A warm winter and early spring were followed by unusually high temperatures during May and June. A good flowering and reasonable conditions led to high hopes for the vintage. Most unfortunately, just as the harvest was due, the heavens opened and it rained virtually non-stop, leading to serious dilution of the quality. No vintage wines, but plenty of average wines for NV.

1994 The same problem as in 1993 affected this year. Following favourable conditions for growth, the vintage prospects looked good. However, yet again some ten days before the harvest was due, heavy rain struck the area leading to dilution in quality.

Reasonable quality NV wines were made by those who selected their grapes very carefully.

1995 After the previous four harvests, where all too often great promise had been destroyed by rain, this harvest brought welcome relief. Growing conditions were generally good throughout, although a little rot did develop and the picking in good conditions of healthy grapes gave good wines for NV blending together with some high-quality vintage ones.

1996 Following good sunny growing conditions, this vintage produced grapes with unusually high sugar contents but also a strong level of acidity, a combination rarely seen. The quality of the *vins clairs*, most particularly Chardonnay, was outstanding, and this is a year for great, well-balanced, long-lived wines.

1997 A year where great pessimism at the end of July gave way to amazement. Severe frosts in early January, followed by three abnormally dry months and very cold nights in April, left weakened vines which were attacked by mildew. Then the sun came out and a hot August stopped the mildew. The grapes ripened well and not a single drop of rain fell during the harvest. At present, it is expected to be a good vintage year.

APPENDIX 6

Premiers Crus

99%
Mareuil-sur-Aÿ
Tauxières

95%
Bergères-les-Vertus
Billy-le-Grand
Bisseuil
Chouilly**
Cuis*
Dizy
Grauves*
Trepail
Vaudemanges
Vertus
Villeneuve-Renneville
Villers-Marmery
Voipreux

94%
Chigny-les-Roses
Cormontreuil
Ludes
Montbre
Rilly-la-Montagne
Taissy
Trois-Puits

93%
Avenay
Champillon
Cumières
Hautvillers
Mutigny

90%
Bezannes
Chamery
Coligny*
Cuis**
Ecueil
Etrechy*
Grauves**
Jouy-les-Reims
Pargny-les-Reims
Pierry
Sacy
Tours-sur-Marne*
Villedommange
Villers-Allerand
Villers-aux-Noeuds

(NB: Where a village is named twice, it is rated differently for different grapes.)

** Black grapes only. * White grapes only. Chouilly and Tours-sur-Marne are also grands crus, but different grapes.

Glossary

À la glace One method of *dégorgement*. The bottle neck, holding the unwanted sediment, is immersed in a frozen brine solution.

À la volée *Dégorgement* effected manually, from the French phrase meaning 'to catch in mid-air'. The expression derives from the report made by the released sediment.

Assemblage 'Assembling': the blending of base wines to make the final *cuvée*. It is the quality and character of the blended base wines that determine the quality of the finished product.

Atmospheres 1 atmosphere is equivalent to 15 pounds per square inch of pressure.

Autolysis The enzymatic destruction of cells; in the case of champagne, the action of the dead yeasts, or lees, after the second fermentation.

Bentonite First discovered in Fort Benton, Wyoming, this montmorillonite clay is a hydrated compound of aluminium and silicon oxides which, when combined with water, is a strong absorber and is therefore useful for the clarification of grape must, generally of white wines. Also used for *fining*; see next page.

Blanc de blancs From white grapes only; in the case of champagne, from 100 per cent Chardonnay.

Blanc de noirs From black grapes only; in the case of champagne, from the two Pinots.

Botrytis The viticultural manifestation of *Botrytis fuckelinia* is defined as *Botrytis cinerea* and can also occur in a benevolent form, weather conditions permitting, giving what is known as Noble Rot and resulting in some of the greatest sweet wines. Wearing its sinister mask, this is the fungus, grey rot, which affects damaged or unripe grapes, or occurs in humid conditions, and is a particular hazard if there is persistent rainfall close to the harvest. Grape varieties which give dense bunches with a high sugar reading are the most prone, Pinot Noir being among them. Green pruning around the fruit and canopy management are deterrents, as is the use of chemicals. The last, however, seems to be the least effective as grey rot rapidly learns how to cope with fungicides.

Boues de ville   'The refuse of the town.' After appropriate treatment, it is utilised as a fertiliser in the vineyards, lending the distinctive flashes of shredded blue plastic to the landscape.

Buyer's Own Brand (BOB)   See **Marque d'acheteur**.

Chaufferettes   The paraffin burners used to create a source of heat in the vineyards and thus attenuate the hazards of frost.

Chlorosis   A condition, the result of a dearth of iron or other nutrients in soils with a high limestone content. Owing to a lack of chlorophyll, the vine's foliage gradually turns yellow. Lime-tolerant rootstocks help to alleviate the problem.

Coopérative Manipulante (CM)   A co-operative making and marketing champagne.

Coulure   A malfunction of the vine which may occur if the flowering takes place in the wrong climatic conditions, such as cloudy, cold and wet weather. The sap then travels to the stalks rather than the fruit and the development of the berries is retarded, resulting in a reduced harvest.

Courtier   A wine broker.

Crayère   A Gallo-Roman chalk pit. In Reims these retain the ideal temperatures for the storage of wine and are so used. Some, such as those owned by Ruinart and Pommery (with its fascinating carvings) are essential sights for the visitor to the area.

Cru   The 'growth'. The wine from a specific village or commune.

Cuvée   From '*cuve*' meaning vat or tank. The blend of base wines amassed for second fermentation in bottle. For another meaning, see **Taille**.

Débourbage   The settling or separation of must, after pressing, from solid matter before fermentation.

Dégorgement   The disgorging or discharging of the deposit in the champagne bottle after riddling or *remuage*.

Deuxièmes tailles   See **Taille**. NB This has now been abolished in Champagne.

Dosage   The *liqueur d'expédition*. The mixture of wine and sugar syrup which may be added to the bottle of champagne, to soften the wine, after *dégorgement*. The *dosage* adjusts the level of sweetness or residual sugar in the finished wine.

Downy mildew   Also known as *Peronospera*, this fungal disease is caused by the *Plasmopara viticola* organism. Originating from American vines in 1878, the disease has now spread internationally, apart from a few areas. Downy mildew assails the green parts of vines and the leaf loss reduces photosynthesis, thus delaying ripening, and depresses carbohydrates, making the plant more susceptible to the winter chill. First seen as 'oil spots' on the leaves, which then develop white 'downy' growths on their bases, the fungus develops under warm and humid conditions. Copper-based sprays provide effective protection, but are short-lasting. Disease-resistant varieties are also being developed.

Échelle des crus The 'scale' or percentage system classifying the *crus* of Champagne.

Épluchage The sorting and selection of fruit in the vineyard (*éplucher* means 'to go over with a fine-tooth comb').

Fanleaf degeneration A network of related viral diseases inducing malformation of the shoots and leaves, causing the latter to assume a fan shape (thus the name). There is no effective control; prevention, through the use of virus-free vines in appropriate soils, is the best cure. Once infected, the vineyard must be grubbed up.

Fining The clarification and stabilisation of the wine, using a fining agent, following fermentation. In Champagne, gelatine or bentonite are generally employed for this purpose.

Grand cru 'Great growth', referring to one of the seventeen villages with a 100 per cent rating in the *échelle des crus*.

Grande Marque 'Great brand.' A major champagne house which belonged to the now disbanded Syndicat des Grandes Marques (founded in 1882 and dissolved in 1997).

Gyropalettes A mechanised riddling system which may be operated manually or by computer. Developed in Catalonia in the 1970s, a specially constructed metal pallet holds up to 500 bottles in a movable frame.

Lees The dregs, or sediment, that settle in the base of the fermentation vessel or bottle. The term *sur lie* refers to a wine which is allowed to maintain contact with its lees and, in the case of bottle-fermented sparkling wine, produces flavour compounds through yeast autolysis.

Liqueur de tirage The addition of sugar and yeast to the blended base wines to trigger a second fermentation in the bottle, thus generating carbon dioxide gas.

Liqueur d'expédition See **Dosage**.

Marque d'acheteur Or **Buyer's Own Brand (BOB)**. The brand name belongs to the wholesale buyer.

Mesoclimate The climate of a particular vineyard site. The term *microclimate* is frequently and incorrectly applied to this large-scale, topographical unit of measurement.

Microclimate A much misused and abused term. A microclimate, viticulturally speaking, is measured in millimetres and refers to the space around each individual vine or even the microzone around component parts of each vine.

Millerandage Inclement weather at flowering may cause defective propagation and result in only partially developed fruit alongside healthy grapes, the small berries being seedless.

Millésime French for 'vintage', thus the year of the vintage.

Millésimé The wine of a single year only – in Champagne, a vintage champagne.

Négociant Manipulant (NM) A Champagne house. The *négociant* (merchant) *manipulant* (handling) may produce some or all of his wine from his own vineyard(s), but is also permitted to purchase grapes or wines from others.

Négociant Non-manipulant Sells champagne under his own name which he has not actually made.

Oidium tuckeri See **Powdery mildew**.

Peronospera See **Downy mildew**.

Pétillant Gently effervescent.

Phylloxera vastatrix or Phylloxera (from the Greek φύλλον, meaning 'leaf', and ξηρός 'dry') 'the devastator'. *Dactylosphaera vitifoliae* is the correct if less evocative name. This aphid or louse arrived from the USA and became the scourge of European viticulture from the 1860s. Phylloxera attacks the root system of the European *vitis vinifera*, eventually destroying the vine. The grafting on to American, non-*vitis vinifera* rootstock became the established method of control. Spread by man, the wind and machine, extermination has proved impossible although certain areas with sandy soils are, thus far, immune.

Plafond limite de classement Literally the upper limit of classification, i.e. the maximum quantity of wine of a given classification that can be made from the declared weight of grapes. If exceeded, and after organoleptic testing, then the wines should be sent for distillation.

Poignetage From the French *poigne*, 'firmhandedness', alternatively from *poignet*, or wrist, meaning a flick of the wrist. The agitation of the bottles during the stacking and unstacking of the bottles resting *sur lattes*, preventing the lees from adhering to the sides.

Powdery mildew Also known as *Oidium tuckeri*, after the Mr Tucker who first identified it in 1845, and as *Uncinula necator*. It has spread internationally, but many native American vines are resistant. As with downy mildew, this fungal disease attacks the green parts of the vine, and the powdery appearance of the infected plant gives it its name. The disease also flourishes in warm conditions (but does not respond to humidity) and can survive the winter onslaught. When bunches are infected the yield is greatly reduced, the fruit failing to achieve full size. Sulphur-based powders and organic fungicides, along with new developments in vine breeding, help to inhibit the disease.

Premier cru 'First growth', referring to one of the villages with a rating of between 90 and 99 per cent in the *échelle des crus*.

Premières tailles See Taille.

Prise de mousse 'Capturing the fizziness.' The process, during the second fermentation, by which the added sugar and yeast *liqueur* is converted into alcohol and carbon dioxide, the latter being released on opening in the form of bubbles or foam.

Punt The indentation at the base of wine bottles.

Pupitre The wooden racks, hinged rectangular boards, used in the process of riddling by hand which follows the *prise de mousse*.

Queue A cask of 96-gallon capacity.

Racking In French, *soutirage*. Part of the clarification and aeration process, this involves the removal of clear wine from the settled sediment in the container by draining the wine into a fresh container.

Récemment dégorgé (RD) 'Recently disgorged.' The initials have been registered as a trademark by Bollinger (although other houses also release this style), and indicate a vintage wine which has only just been disgorged.

Récoltant Coopérateur (RC) *Récolte* means 'harvest'. The *récoltant* is the grower, in this case a small grower who, lacking the necessary equipment, has his wine made by a co-operative and then sells it under his own label. (The grapes may have been blended with others.)

Récoltant Manipulant (RM) A grower who makes his own champagne from his own fruit and is permitted to buy in up to 5 per cent.

Remuage The 'riddling' or 'shaking' of the bottle to dislodge the deposit left in the bottle after second fermentation.

Reserve wines Still wines from earlier vintages than the current and blended in to create the NV house style.

Sur lattes The term may refer either to wines awaiting disgorgement, labelled as the buyer's own product, or to champagnes stored horizontally.

Sur pointes After *remuage*, the stacking of large numbers of bottles, the cork or 'point' in the punt of the bottle beneath.

Taille The French term for 'pruning', from *tailler*, meaning to prune or to cut. The **premières tailles**, actually the second pressings, follow the **cuvée**, the first, and best, 2,050 litres of pressed must. The **premières tailles** give a further 410 litres. The **deuxièmes tailles** or third pressings are no longer permitted, but gave a further 205 litres.

Tête de cuvée The *cuvée*, the highest-quality must from the first pressings.

Véraison The first stage of ripening when the fruit begins to soften, swell and change colour; the sugars accumulate and there is a reduction in acidity.

Vin clair The clear wine obtained after the processes of **racking** and **fining**.

Bibliography

Allen, H. Warner, *A History of Wine*, London, 1961

Arlott, John, *Krug, House of Champagne*, London, 1976

Duijker, Hubrecht, *The Wines of the Loire, Alsace and Champagne*, London, 1983

Edwards, Michael, *The Champagne Companion*, London, 1994

Faith, Nicholas, *The Story of Champagne*, London, 1988

Forbes, Patrick, *Champagne: The Wine, the Land and the People*, London, 1967

Gemeline, Patrick de, *Ruinart*, Paris, 1994

Jullien, André, *Topography of All Known Vineyards*, London, 1824

Macquitty, Jane, *Champagne and Sparkling Wines*, London, 1991

Polignac, Prince Alain de, *Madame Pommery*, Paris, 1994

Ray, Cyril, *Bollinger*, London, 1971

Robinson, Jancis (ed.), *The Oxford Companion to Wine*, Oxford, 1994

Seward, Desmond, *Monks and Wine*, London, 1979

Simon, André, *The History of Champagne*, London, 1962

Stevenson, Tom, *Champagne*, London, 1986

Sutcliffe, Serena, *Champagne*, London, 1988

Taittinger, Claude, *Champagne*, Paris, 1996

Vandyke Price, Pamela, *Guide to the Wines of Champagne*, London, 1979

— *Wine Lore, Legends and Tradition*, London, 1985

Vizetelly, Henry, *A History of Champagne*, London, 1882

Index

INDEX